Airborne Early Warning Aircraft
Wellington to Wedgetail

CHRIS GIBSON

MODERN MILITARY AIRCRAFT SERIES, VOLUME 14

Front cover image: Royal Australian Air Force (RAAF) Boeing 737-7ES/E-7A Wedgetail Airborne Early Warning & Control (AEW&C) aircraft A30-003 (Wedgetail 21) completes a missed approach at Hervey Bay (Fraser Coast) Airport. (John Lee/CQ Plane Spotting)

Title page image: Water vapour trails stream from the tips of the Hamilton Standard propellers of a Grumman E-2C Hawkeye as it departs the flight deck of a US Navy carrier. The Hawkeye is an old design but has remained at the cutting edge of AEW technology and provides the US and French navies with state-of-the-art air and sea surveillance. (DoD/US Navy)

Contents page image: One of the principal lessons from the Falklands War was the need for AEW. Westland, much to the RAF's chagrin, took a modified Searchwater radar from the Nimrod upgrade programme and fitted it in a Sea King. The result was the Sea King AEW2, with XV671 being one of the first production examples. (Blue Envoy Collection)

Back cover image: The antenna of the ACI system's metric radar used a rotating Yagi antenna. The centimetric radars used in subsequent AEW experiments used a rotating dish antenna enclosed in a radome. The ACI Wellington and its dorsal antenna was a portent for the future. (Blue Envoy Collection)

Boeing E-3D Sentry AEW1 ZH106 and Panavia Tornado F3 ZE862 in formation over the North Atlantic. The RAF's Greenland Iceland UK (GIUK) Gap air defence team comprised the Sentry AEW1, Tornado F3 and VC10 tanker. (Blue Envoy Collection)

Published by Key Books
An imprint of Key Publishing Ltd
PO Box 100
Stamford
Lincs PE9 1XQ

www.keypublishing.com

The right of Chris Gibson to be identified as the author of this book has been asserted in accordance with the Copyright, Designs and Patents Act 1988 Sections 77 and 78.

Copyright © Chris Gibson, 2023

ISBN 978 1 80282 674 6

All rights reserved. Reproduction in whole or in part in any form whatsoever or by any means is strictly prohibited without the prior permission of the Publisher.

Typeset by SJmagic DESIGN SERVICES, India.

Contents

Acknowledgements 4
Introduction 5

Chapter 1	An Eye in the Sky..7
Chapter 2	Britain's First Attempts..10
Chapter 3	A Brand-New Cadillac...15
Chapter 4	Replacing Cadillac...18
Chapter 5	Overland..23
Chapter 6	UK AEW – The Baggers...30
Chapter 7	Overland But All At Sea – The RAF and AEW..39
Chapter 8	A New Generation...51
Chapter 9	Bizjet Revolution...54
Chapter 10	Patrolling the Arctic – Soviet AEW..61
Chapter 11	China and India..72
Chapter 12	Useful Clutter – Battlefield Surveillance and Radar Reconnaissance...........76
Conclusion	90

Appendix 1 Radar Basics 91
Appendix 2 FASS and FMICW – Britain's Preference 93
Glossary 94
Bibliography 95

Acknowledgements

As ever, a book such as this has many contributors, even if they only answered one of my daft questions. Much of the research for this title was carried out over more than two decades and included trips to the numerous BAE Systems archives including Warton, Brough and Woodford. The many volunteers who tend these archives are the unsung heroes of aviation writing, so many thanks to Tony Wilson, Paul Lawson, George Jenks, and their colleagues around the country. Material relating to Vickers' work in the Airborne Early Warning (AEW) field is held at Brooklands Museum and was diligently dug out for me by Albert Kitchenside and, of course, Chris Farara. Tony Pilmer, Librarian at the National Aerospace Library at Farnborough, appears to view my requests as challenges and invariably meets, if not exceeds, them.

Since my knowledge of radar and its inner workings is less than extensive, great reliance was placed on those that do know. David Mackenzie has, for decades, been my first point of contact on radar matters and his guidance has been crucial to my understanding of radar since the last millennium.

On the American aspects of AEW, Robert Hopkins and his many contacts proved invaluable. Robert may even be coming around to the outlandish idea that AEW was a British invention. On the Soviet/Russian front, Yefim Gordon and Dimitry Kommissarov provided the most up-to-date information and many photos. Much of the information on China's efforts in the field originate with Andreas Ruprecht whose work on demystifying Chinese aviation is outstanding. His level-headed and objective approach to sorting the wheat from the chaff (or should that be the return from the clutter?) is lauded by all.

The production and editing team at Key Publishing, particularly Commissioning Editor Brianne Bellio and text editors Francesca Studholme-Smith and Bernadette Hewitt are always a joy to work with. Lastly, I must thank Ian Shaw. His passion and knowledge on the subject of airborne early warning knows no bounds and this work would not have been possible without Ian's help.

Chris Gibson, Washington,
June 2023

Introduction

In the period following the Russia invasion of Ukraine in February 2022, if you fired up a virtual radar on a computer or smart phone and moved the focus to Eastern Europe, a remarkable picture appeared. Aside from transport aircraft and tankers, one aircraft type was omnipresent on NATO's eastern border – AEW aircraft. These included the United States Air Force (USAF) and NATO Boeing E-3A, E-3C/G Sentry fleet, France's E-3F Sentry, Turkish Air Force Boeing E-7s and Italian Air Force Gulfstream G550CAEW. These aircraft are monitoring the airspace over Ukraine and Belarus, passing what they see to the relevant command structure, aiding decision making and possibly providing early warning of missile attacks.

The importance of this capability, now called 'battlespace management', can be summed up in a single example due to its omission – the lack of airborne early warning made the recovery of the Falkland Islands in 1982 much more difficult. The lessons of the Falklands conflict did not go unheeded and from being in the order of battle of Israel, UK, USA and USSR in 1980, by the end of the 20th century AEW aircraft were in service with air forces across the world. Long derided as mere support acts for the fighters and bombers, the truth is that a modern air force equipped with the latest generation of multirole combat aircraft cannot operate to its optimum capacity without AEW.

An earlier conflict, Vietnam, showed the importance of AEW in offensive operations, with College Eye Lockheed EC-121 Warning Stars in conjunction with Red Crown US naval vessels and ground facilities directing US fighters against North Vietnamese interceptors. Developmental work towards replacing the Warning Star led to the E-3 Sentry that would become the epitome of battlespace management in the post-1990 period of expeditionary warfare.

Since the turn of the century, the range of AEW platforms available has multiplied, a proliferation made possible by the shrinking size of the hardware, radar and computers, and the increased capability of that hardware. Despite this, until the 2020s, these platforms had to be large enough to accommodate

Something old, something new, something blue (and old). Two No 8 Sqn Sentry AEW1s flank a Shackleton AEW2, possibly at Waddington in the early 1990s. Five years separate the first flights of the Shackleton MR2 and the Boeing 707 (pictured), and the differences show the pace of aircraft development in the 1950s. (via NELSAM)

AEW aircraft have never been pretty, but the head-on view of the Erieye EMB-145H AEW&C tends to support that belief. This Hellenic Air Force example shows the cooling intake on the antenna and the additional vertical fins on the tailplane. (Anthony Mylonakis via Ioannis Mylonas)

a crew, but in what is effectively a return to the 1945 Project Cadillac (the secret project that produced flying radar), the Gulfstream G550CAEW aircraft may soon be the first AEW aircraft without operators.

Why was this essential role developed and why did it take so long for aircraft to appear in the role? There are various reasons, but essentially it refers to the landscape clutter and the increasing sophistication of computer power. This work is intended as a description of the many AEW platforms from the early days of 'follow-my-leader' to the latest autonomous platforms flying in a racetrack pattern at high altitude. Look elsewhere for details on radars, wavelengths, pulse repetition frequencies and war stories, as these are available in the more comprehensive volumes on the subject. This volume is all about the platforms that have been designed and come to fruition and their histories.

Chapter 1
An Eye in the Sky

Tally ho! – The traditional cry made by the huntsman to tell the field that quarry has been sighted.

From the beginnings of air combat over the Western Front in the first year of the Great War, some form of organisation of aircraft in combat was required. Flight or Squadron Leaders, brightly coloured streamer fluttering from an interplane strut, would guide the other pilots and their aircraft against the enemy in what was pretty much a follow-the-leader process. France's Armée de l'Air sought to improve this and with the advent of aircraft radios in the 1930s, developed a version of the three-seat Potez 631 that carried a Commandant à la Chasse (fighter controller). Flying above the air battle, this co-ordinating officer could look down on the air battle and direct aircraft as required. This could only be described as the worst job in the air force as keeping track of the ensuing mêlée was difficult.

Eventually the Armée de l'Air dropped the idea. Interestingly, the concept was adopted by RAF Bomber Command, with the Master Bomber, a senior officer who would fly above the target and broadcast orders or drop more target markers. Group Captain Leonard Cheshire VC pioneered the technique and became synonymous with the role, eventually using de Havilland Mosquitos or, in Cheshire's case, a North American P-51 Mustang 'acquired' from the US 8th Air Force.

Once radios became commonplace in fighter aircraft in the 1940s, the formation commanders could co-ordinate engagements. The game-changer, however, was ground-controlled interception using radar,

The fighter controllers of the Great War were the Wing Leaders. Identified by a streamer or flag fluttering from an interplane strut, as seen on this Sopwith Camel, the rest of the Wing followed their leader wherever they went. (Via Dave Birch)

No matter how good, no matter how powerful, no matter where they are sited, ground radars such as this Marconi Martello S713 (AMES Type 90) are restricted by their 'radar horizon'. From the first application of radar in air defence, pilots learned to avoid detection by flying low, below the radar horizon. The answer was to place the radar as high as possible – in an aircraft. (Blue Envoy Collection)

which made for a formidable defence system. This combination of ground control and radar in the form of the Filter Room together with Chain Home radar stations employed by the RAF in the Battle of Britain saw Fighter Command see off a much bigger foe.

A similar system, Himmelbett, was employed by the Luftwaffe against the RAF during the bomber offensive against Germany with one control centre controlling a night-fighter and directing it onto a bomber. The Himmelbett centres formed a chain along the western region of occupied Europe called the Kammhuber Line.

The Luftwaffe and RAF relied on ground radars for their command-and-control systems with radar becoming essential warfighting equipment on both sides by 1941. Radar, however, did have a significant limitation – the horizon. Radar 'sees' in straight lines by using a transmitter to emit a pulse of radio frequency (RF) energy which travels outwards, hits a target and returns to a receiver. The time taken equates to distance and the direction of the 'return' gives the bearing from the radar. While that is a much simplified description, straight lines of the radar beam are limited to line of sight by the curvature of the Earth, which gave rise to the radar horizon, below which the radar could not detect targets. All an attacking aircraft had to do to avoid detection was fly below the radar horizon for as long as possible, a tactic that has been used since radar became viable during World War Two.

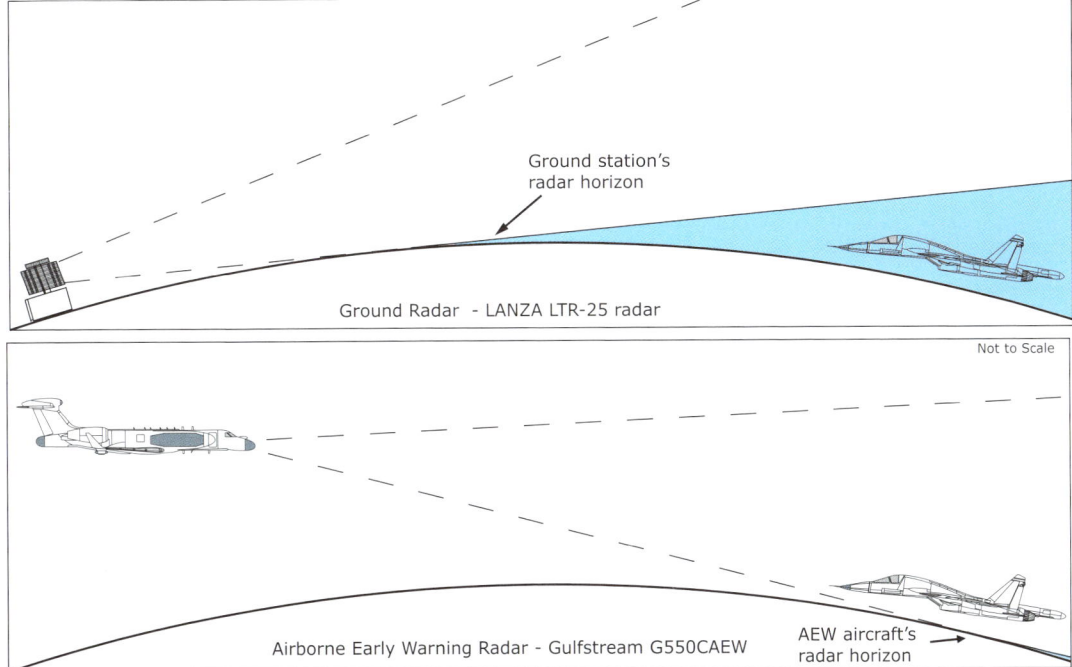

The radar horizon is due to the curvature of the earth and the distance of the radar to the horizon increases with altitude. This diagram shows how a low-flying strike aircraft can be detected much earlier by the AEW platform than the ground-based early warning radar. (Author)

Chapter 2
Britain's First Attempts

'H2S [radar] gave us a good picture of the ground below us, and it was a pity it couldn't give us a good picture of the aeroplanes around us'. Wg Cdr Dudley Saward, Bomber Command liaison officer at TRE, to Bernard Lovell, TRE.

Radar horizon is determined by height; a person standing on a beach has a visual horizon three miles (5km), but by climbing a hill to 100ft (30m), the horizon of that person expands to 12 miles (19km) away. Radar developers used this knowledge at the Telecommunications Research Establishment (TRE) and, by spring 1942, had installed a modified Air-to-Surface Vessel (ASV) Mk.II radar, as used by maritime patrol aircraft, in Vickers Wellington Ic R1629. The most obvious change to the Wellington was the 15ft (4.2m) long rotating Yagi antenna installed above the fuselage. The system, known as Airborne Controlled Interception (ACI), worked well, ultimately ushering in the advent of the cavity magnetron and centimetric wavelength radars that device made possible, superseded metric radars such as the 5ft 5in (1.7m) wavelength used by ASV Mk.II. Once the metric wavelength radars were deemed obsolete (although they did have their uses) and despite a successful trial with Fighter Command, the ACI Wellington was stripped of the radar equipment and returned to service as a bomber. The ACI Wellington appeared on the scene at the wrong time, not only was metric radar old hat, but the RAF was going on the offensive.

Centimetric radar became the preferred choice for airborne applications in Allied aircraft. By 1943, it was being used by night fighters and in air-to-surface applications such as the ASV Mk.X on

Vickers Wellington Ic R1629 was fitted with a dorsal rotating antenna for its ASV Mk.II. The Air Controlled Interception (ACI) system was a victim of technological progress. (Blue Envoy Collection)

Inside the ACI Wellington, the radar returns were displayed on the cathode ray tube. Like all early radar systems, interpretation of the display required skill and an additional specialist operator on the crew. (Blue Envoy Collection)

Coastal Command aircraft, but more famously in the H2S ground-mapping radar in Bomber Command's Lancasters and Halifaxes. Wing Commander Saward had, in passing, asked Bernard Lovell if H2S could provide a picture of the aircraft as well as the ground. Interestingly, while operating H2S over Germany, radio operators on RAF bombers had noticed that other aircraft below and around their aircraft did indeed show up on the H2S display. On reporting this phenomenon, it was put to use by TRE which, working under the direction of Bernard Lovell, installed a second display called Fishpond. This display allowed the radio operator to look for other bombers in the stream and avoid collision, allowing closer formations, and could also identify German night fighters in good time to give a warning to the pilot and gunners. The system's range could be extended by banking the aircraft to 'see' what was flying to the side of the aircraft as well as below.

Bomber Command was not alone in discovering that aircraft showed up on the scopes of its air-to-surface radars. Having cancelled the metric wavelength ACI system in favour of the advanced centimetric system, Coastal Command also noticed that aircraft showed up on its ASV radar displays. The most significant application of this aspect was Operation *Cork*, conducted on 5/6 June 1944 and intended to screen the invasion fleet as it crossed the Channel for the *Overlord* landings.

The aim of *Cork* was to prevent German vessels; E-boats, submarines, and other surface elements from getting 'in about' the fleet and causing the havoc that had been wreaked by E-boats at Slapton Sands during Operation *Tiger* in April 1944. The aircraft involved in *Cork* could also detect German aircraft such as Junkers Ju 88 long-range fighters based in western France, and direct Allied fighters to intercept them.

On a more aggressive theme, Operation *Vapour* was carried out in late 1944/early 1945 and involved a Wellington GR Mk XIV fitted with a modified ASV Mk VI radar and carrying a fighter controller. Operation *Vapour* was the first airborne early warning and control (AEW&C) system, which the RAF called Airborne Warning and Interception (AWI). *Vapour* involved the AWI Wellington and two Mosquito NF.XVIIIs hunting down Heinkel He 111H-22s that were launching Fieseler Fi 103 (V-1) flying bombs against targets in the English Midlands during Operation *Rumpelkammer*. In a further pointer to the future, the Wellington/Mosquito trio were directed to their patrol areas by *Ultra* intelligence gleaned from German Enigma traffic, intercepted by the RAF's Y-Service and decrypted by Bletchley Park before being forwarded to Fighter Command. All went well in trials, with 38 out of

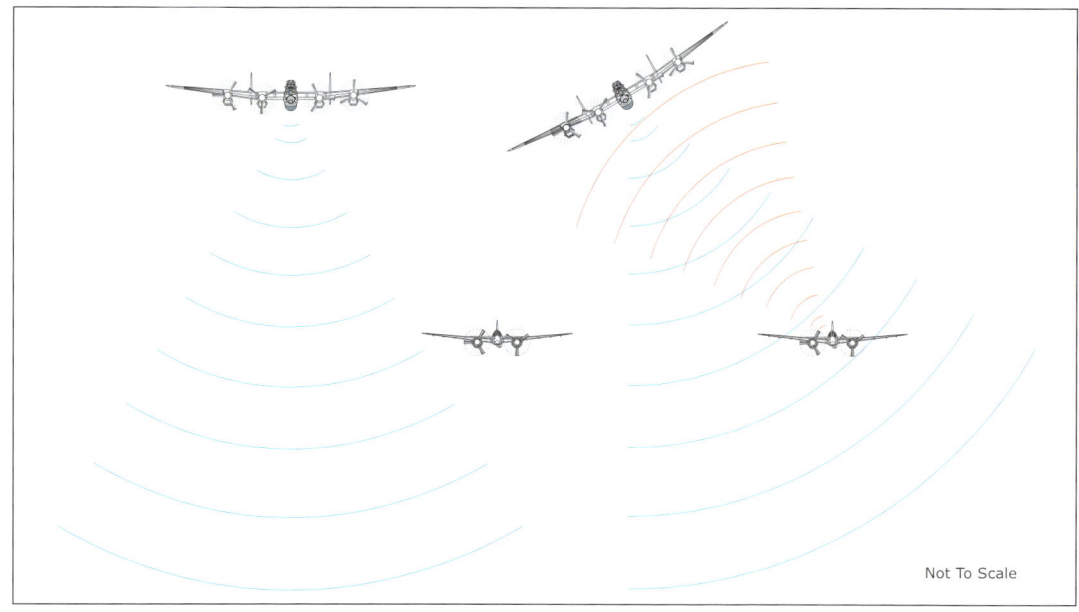

Not To Scale

Above: The Fishpond modification allowed the H2S ground-mapping radar to be used to detect nearby aircraft. By banking the aircraft, the detection range of the system could be increased, giving warning of approaching fighters or other bombers. Fishpond was to be further developed into the Big Picture, but the end of the war saw its development cancelled. (Author)

Left: The ventral bulge between the wing and the tailplane of this Avro Lancaster is the radome for the H2S radar. By the end of the war, most Lancasters were so fitted. This example, NX612, is a BVII FE intended for use in the Far East, specifically the preparatory raids for the invasion of Japan and operating under the watchful eye of the Boeing PB-1W or even the RAF's Big Picture. (Crown Copyright via Tony Buttler)

40 trial interceptions against RAF bombers deemed successful, but the night that Vapour went 'live' the Luftwaffe ceased air launching V-1s at Britain, bringing Operations *Rumpelkammer* and *Vapour* to an end.

Had the air war continued beyond 1945, the Air Staff and TRE had plans for what they called the 'Big Picture', which involved fitting three radars in a Boeing C-97 Stratofreighter, but this was cancelled in the postwar rundown of military projects. Big Picture involved major modifications to the Stratofreighter, including removing the entire nose section and replacing it with a radome. The cockpit was moved to the top of the fuselage, with double bubble canopies as used on the Douglas C-124 Globemaster I, which could make landing interesting. In addition to the front-facing main radar, the Horizontal Looker, and Upward and Downward Looker radars were fitted in dorsal and ventral positions. If, as would become standard on AEW aircraft, all-round coverage was required, a radar could be mounted in the tail, in

The radar platform for Operation *Vapour* was the Wellington GR Mk.XIV. This was one of the last Wellington maritime variants and for *Vapour*, the Wellington was fitted with ASV Mk.VI and the latest fighter control systems such as Lucero beacon interrogators to track the Mosquito night fighters. (Blue Envoy Collection)

An Operation *Vapour* interception involved Wellington GR Mk.XIV and a pair of Mosquito night fighters using information from *Ultra* sources to be in the right place at the right time. Once the fighter controller on board the Wellington had detected the V1-carrying Heinkel He 111, the controller directed a Mosquito towards it until the Mosquito's AI radar detected the Heinkel. (Author)

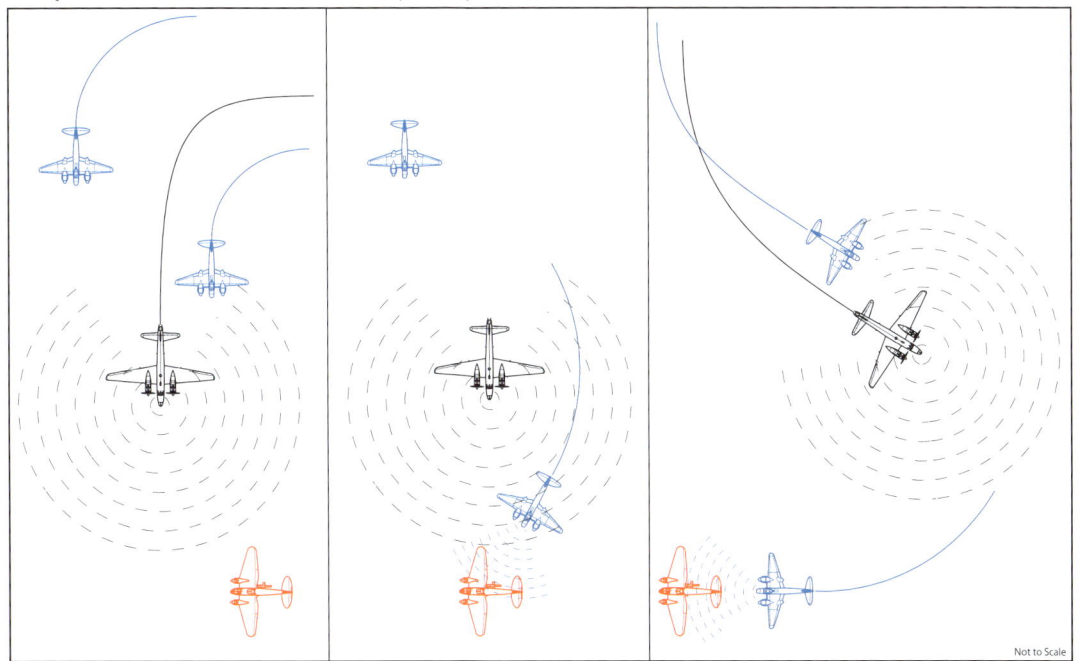

what would have been the first fore-and-aft antenna system (FASS), of which more later. Big Picture was intended to allow co-ordination and direction of bombing raids and provide an onboard commander with an overall view of a raid and, like Fishpond, allow concentration of the main force.

One programme that did survive, for a short period at least, was the AWI Hamilcar that involved a General Aircraft Hamilcar X (powered version of the tank-carrying glider), LA728, fitted with a Plexiglass nose that covered a 7ft (2.1m) diameter dish for a modified ASV Mk.VI. Trials were never going to be

In late 1944, the RAF was looking at the newly developed XC-97 Stratofreighter as the basis for its Big Picture AEW platform. The entire cockpit area would have been replaced by a radome, with dorsal, ventral and tail radomes added for all-round coverage. The Stratofreighter (bottom) and Constellation (top) were the most modern transports available at the end of the war. The Constellation would form the basis of the Warning Star series of AEW aircraft. (Blue Envoy Collection)

satisfactory; the Hamilcar X was underpowered and it was restricted to operating less than 20 miles (32km) offshore. This restriction meant that it suffered from ground clutter from coastal features and while looking promising, plans to fit the system in a Bristol Freighter came to nothing in austerity Britain.

It was all quiet on the AEW front in postwar Britain until 1948 when a US Navy PB-1W and its Cadillac system (see Chapter 3) were assessed at RAF St Eval during Operation *Haddock* in June 1948. The aim of *Haddock* was to evaluate Cadillac against the British Vickers Warwick Mk.V fitted with ASV 13 radar and determine whether the system could be used for a variety of tasks, including 'distant shadowing of ship, fighter control and strike direction'. The RAF found that the AN/APS-20B radar wasn't particularly suited to the RAF's needs. That was indeed true, as the RAF operated mainly over land, be it around the Empire or in Western Europe, and the AN/APS-20 radar suffered from reflections off the landscape and features with in it. Called 'ground clutter' this would afflict airborne radars, their development, capability, and application for the next two decades.

Post-war AEW research saw a modified ASV Mk VI fitted to a Hamilcar X. Underpowered, the Hamilcar was unsuitable for the work, which soon fell by the wayside. (Blue Envoy Collection)

Chapter 3
A Brand-New Cadillac

'The most valuable cargo ever brought to our shores.' James Phinney Baxter III, Director of the US Office of Strategic Services, 1941, describing the items that accompanied the Tizard Mission in September 1940.

Meanwhile in America, having taken delivery of a cavity magnetron provided by the Tizard Mission, the British envoys who visited the US to share radar research and development, the American radar companies and research establishments such as the Massachusetts Institute of Technology Radiation Laboratory (MIT-RL) put centimetric radar to good use in a variety of applications. MIT had developed an S-band (2-4 GigaHertz) snorkel-detecting radar for use in anti-submarine warfare (ASW) that was manufactured by the Hazeltine Corporation as the AN/APS-20 and fitted to carrier-borne ASW aircraft such as Grumman TBM Avengers. Given that the RAF had been using ASW radars to detect and direct fighter aircraft since 1941, the logical application for AN/APS-20 was AEW. It would be the start of a decades-long service in that role.

Known as Project Cadillac (named after a mountain in Maine, not the car), the AN/APS-20 in the AEW role could extend the range of the fleet's radar coverage to provide early warning of enemy attacks, or direction of airstrikes and air combat by friendly aircraft. It was a useful capability but when Japanese aircraft started to dive onto US Navy ships in October 1944, Project Cadillac gained added impetus as the Kamikaze suicide bombers were best tackled by fighter aircraft long before they approached the fleet. The AN/APS-20 was modified to become an airborne radar picket that provided longer range than the existing picket destroyers. What arose from Project Cadillac was the Hazeltine AN/APS-20A radar with an 8 x 4ft (2.44 x 1.22m) antenna installed in the weapons bay of a Grumman TBM-3 Avenger, becoming the TBM-3W that entered service in February 1945, the first AEW aircraft to enter squadron service.

The first dedicated AEW aircraft to become operational was the Grumman TB3W Avenger with the Cadillac system. These carried the AN/APS-20 radar to altitude and, lacking the space for controllers, transmitted the radar picture to the carrier and other ships using a system called Bellhop. (Blue Envoy Collection)

Since the Avenger lacked the space for a controller, the radar picture was transmitted via a television system called 'Bellhop' to the carrier's combat information centre for analysis, with the TBM-3W acting as a high-altitude antenna that extended the ship's radar horizon.

In preparation for the invasion of Japan named Operation *Downfall*, the US Navy sought a machine with longer range that was more capable and could operate from land bases such as Okinawa, the intended base for fighter operations during *Downfall*. The AN/APS-20B radar, differing from the A-model by having a larger antenna, was installed in US Navy PB-1W bombers (Douglas-built Boeing B-17s), which also benefitted from carrying a fighter controller. The AN/APS-20 radar went from strength to strength and was installed on the Douglas Skyraider, Grumman AF-2W Guardian and Lockheed's P-2 Neptune, with the latter two as ASW radars.

The US Navy sought an improvement on the PB-1W and from 1949 the AN/APS-20 was fitted with a much larger antenna and installed in a ventral radome on the Lockheed L-749 Constellation, which the Navy initially designated the PO-1W, later changed to WV-1. In 1952, the system was installed in the L-1049 Super Constellation as the PO-2W, which was redesignated as the WV-2 in 1954. The AN/APS-20 radar was soon replaced with the AN/APS-95 radar to improve performance in what became the EC-121D. Between 1954 and 1965, US Navy WV-2s operated off the East and West coasts of the United States and Canada as BARLANT (Atlantic coast) and BARPAC (Pacific coast) to extend the east and west range of the Distant Early Warning (DEW) Line of radar stations used to detect incoming Soviet bombers. These patrols were later extended to cover the Greeland Iceland UK (GIUK) Gap to the Atlantic and between Midway and the Aleutians in the Pacific.

The USAF received ten WV-2s transferred from the Navy in 1953, which it designated the RC-121C. Subsequently 74 EC-121D Warning Stars were procured by the USAF. In 1962, with the standardisation of military aircraft designation, the US Navy and USAF AEW variants of the Super Constellation were designated EC-121s or variations, depending on the specific role for which they were manufactured.

From 1967, the USAF's Warning Stars operated in the South East Asian theatre providing AEW and conducting more specialised surveillance tasks. Although 1967 saw the AEW Warning Stars commence operations in Vietnam, other variants of the airframe had already served in specialist reconnaissance roles,

At one point in the mid-1960s the RAF considered acquiring the Lockheed EC-121H Warning Star but its lack of overland capability persuaded the RAF to continue with its own overland radar programme. (Terry Panopalis Collection)

such as the EC-121R Batcat that monitored movements on the Ho Chi Minh trail. For the AEW role, programmes such as Big Eye and College Eye monitored North Vietnamese MiGs and provided warnings to US strike aircraft. Vietnam pushed the EC-121 and its AN/APS-95 surveillance radar and AN/APS-45 height-finding radar to the limit as these had been designed to operate over the sea. Operating over land was fraught with problems caused by ground clutter and a number of 'workarounds' were developed, but the problem was never completely solved. The experience in Vietnam showed that a new airborne warning and control system was required to replace the piston-engined Warning Stars.

Intended to support air operations over and around the Japanese Home Islands during Operation *Downfall*, the Boeing PB-1W entered service just after the war and provided land-based AEW cover for the US Navy. This example, having its engines serviced, belonged to VW-1 at Naval Air Station (NAS) Barbers Point in 1953. (Blue Envoy Collection)

The Lockheed Constellation formed the basis of both US Navy and US Air Force (USAF) AEW platforms. This image of EC-121 Warning Star, 13838, shows the dorsal AN/APS-45 height-finding and the ventral radome for the AN/APS-20 antenna. The Warning Stars monitored the airspace of the East and West coasts of the North American continent. (Blue Envoy Collection)

Chapter 4
Replacing Cadillac

Hawkeye – A person with keen eyesight or one who is especially observant.
(*Oxford English Dictionary*)

To replace the carrier-borne Grumman TBM-3Ws, the US Navy fitted the AN/APS-20A radar (subsequently replaced with the AN/APS-20F version) to the Douglas AD-4 Skyraider attack aircraft, to produce the AD-4W. Unlike the TBM-3Ws, the AD-4W was fitted out with a cabin in the fuselage to accommodate two operators who provided a control function and allowed a strike package to have AEW support away from the carrier. Some 158 AD-4Ws entered service from 1948 and conducted missions during the Korean War in support of United Nations (UN) operations. The Fleet Air Arm was provided with 50 examples of the AD-4W from 1951, with these being designated as Skyraider AEW1.

The AD-4W served with the US Navy until replaced by the Grumman WF Tracer (colloquially known as the 'Willy Fudd' even after being redesignated E-1 in 1962) from 1958. Based on the Grumman C-2 Trader carrier onboard delivery (COD) type, itself derived from the Grumman S-2 Tracker ASW aircraft. The E-1 Tracer carried a crew of four, including two radar/intercept officers and carried a Hazeltine AN/APS-82 radar in a large dorsal fairing that dominated the aircraft. The size of the radome prompted a complete redesign of the Trader's empennage, changing from a single fin to three 'fins' on the Tracer, although one of these fins was effectively a pylon to support the rear of the radome.

In service for nearly 60 years, the Grumman E-2 Hawkeye is probably the most successful AEW aircraft to date. Operated from aircraft carriers by the US and French navies, it has also been operated from land by Egypt, Israel, Japan, Mexico, Singapore and Taiwan. It has no obvious replacement in the carrier-borne role. (Blue Envoy Collection)

To replace the TB3W Avenger, the US Navy opted for the Douglas AD Skyraider. This example, 137560, is one of the later AD-6 variants of VA-85 embarked on USS *Forrestal*. (Blue Envoy Collection)

In addition to the ventral radome for the AN/APS-20 radar, the conversion of the Skyraider to the AEW role included a compartment for two operators in the mid fuselage. This example is one of 50 AD4Ws transferred to the Royal Navy. (Blue Envoy Collection)

The AN/APS-82 radar featured an important innovation in AEW – an airborne moving target indicator (AMTI) that allowed aircraft returns to be identified in the clutter from surface returns. Clutter had been one of the major obstacles to the development of 'overland' AEW aircraft and one of the main reasons for the US Navy taking the lead in AEW until the late 1970s when radar and computer technologies matured enough to deal with clutter. An AMTI in its most basic form compared the current radar scan 'picture' with the previous scan's picture and if a fast-moving aircraft is 'in' the picture, it will have moved position, whereas ground or sea returns – the clutter – will be the same and can be filtered out and rejected. In the 1950s, hardware as basic as a Chinagraph pencil and a Perspex overlay would provide the 'clutter rejection'. As computing power increased, software for signal processing was developed providing the next leap in AEW technology.

The replacement for the WF/E-1 Tracer incorporated gas turbine power with a feature last seen on Wellington R1629 in 1942 – a rotating dorsal antenna. The Grumman E-2 Hawkeye has the distinction of being the only aircraft designed from scratch for the AEW role and, having entered US Navy service in 1964, is currently approaching 60 years in service. Powered by a pair of Allison T56-425 turboprops rated at 4,600shp (3,430kW) it was initially equipped with the AN/APS-96 radar. The antenna for Hawkeye's radar is installed in a dorsal rotodome, a flat disk-like fairing that provides a uniform aerodynamic shape for the antenna as it rotates, avoiding 'cyclic drag'.

The E-2A and B used the AN/APS-96 radar that was continuously updated until the E-2C, a major systems improvement designated Group 0, was introduced in 1973. The E-2C Group 0 was fitted with the AN/APS-120 radar and systems that integrated the Hawkeye with the aircraft carrier and Grumman F-14 Tomcat, making the US Navy's iconic air defence team of the 1980s. The E-2C was also updated with the Group I fitted with upgraded T56-427 engines, rated at 5,100shp (3,803kW), which significantly improved the E-2C's performance. The AN/APS-125 radar was introduced from 1978. The definitive Group II E-2C appeared in the early 1990s and was fitted with AN/APS-139 and subsequently the AN/APS-145 radar for the Hawkeye 2000 programme from 1997.

In addition to the AN/APS-145 radar, Hawkeye 2000 introduced improved computing power and cooling systems, greatly enhancing the type's combat information centre and co-ordination capability. All these improvements brought a highly advanced battlespace management into the naval air warfare sphere making the US Navy's surveillance capability second to none.

The E-2C Hawkeye has served as a land-based AEW system with several air forces for many years including Egypt, Israel, Japan, Mexico, Singapore and Taiwan, with Israel adding an in-flight refuelling probe decades before the US Navy. The Israeli Air Force received its first Daya (kite) in 1978 and used the aircraft to good effect over the Bekaa Valley in Lebanon during operations in 1982. One very satisfied user of the Hawkeye is France, which has operated the type on the carriers of the Marine National since the 1980s. The Marine National has also upgraded its E-2Cs with the latest systems and one example has been fitted with the eight-blade propellers used on the E-2D.

The Grumman E-1B Tracer provided the US Navy with a much improved capability when it was introduced in 1958. The antenna for its Hazeltine AN/APS-82 was mounted in a large dorsal radome and the radar was the first to feature an Airborne Moving Target Indicator. Intended as a stopgap pending the deployment of the Hawkeye, the Tracer remained in service until 1977. (Terry Panopalis Collection)

From the mid-1970s the Hawkeye worked in tandem with its Grumman stablemate the F-14 Tomcat to provide air defence for the US Navy's carrier groups. This E-2C Hawkeye VAW-120 and F-14B Tomcat VF-32 were both operating from the USS *John F Kennedy*. (Blue Envoy Collection)

After a MiG-25 *Foxbat* defected to Japan in 1976, the Japanese Air Self-Defense Force (JASDF) decided to purchase an AEW aircraft and opted for the E-2C Hawkeye. This example, 54-3458, is on the strength of 601 Sqn JASDF. (Blue Envoy Collection)

Such is the success of the Hawkeye that rather than replace it, the US Navy has invested heavily in an extensive upgrade that included the AN/APY-9 radar on the E-2D Advanced Hawkeye. The APY-9 is an active electronically scanned array (AESA) radar that uses electronic scanning in addition to rotation of the rotodome. The E-2D is compatible with the US Navy's Electromagnetic Aircraft Launch System (EMALS) to be used on its new generation of carriers. Despite using the same basic engine, the E-2D features new eight-bladed propellers on its T-56s, now designated Rolls-Royce/Allison T-56-427A. The E-2D's analogue cockpit has been replaced with a digital glass version and, after 50 years of service, the Hawkeye finally acquired an in-flight refuelling probe.

Existing users of the E-2C, specifically France, are aiming to acquire the E-2D, while the Indian Navy may procure the latest Hawkeye for carrier and land-based operations. It appears that the only replacement for a carrier-borne Hawkeye is another Hawkeye, and the type looks destined to serve for many years to come. If, as Oscar Wilde said: 'Imitation is the sincerest form of flattery' the Russian Yakovlev Yak-44E and Chinese Xi'an KJ-600 that share the Hawkeye's configuration suggest that Grumman and Westinghouse got it right.

Singapore operated the E-2C Hawkeye from 1987 until 2012. This example served with No 111 Sqn at Tengah. It is now displayed at the Republic of Singapore Air Force (RSAF) Museum next to Paya Lebar Air Base. (Author)

The US Navy has operated the widest range of AEW platforms, beginning with Cadillac in 1945. It also operates the last word in naval AEW – Hawkeye. (Author)

Chapter 5
Overland

> Clutter – a collection of things lying about in an untidy state. (*Oxford English Dictionary*)

While the US Navy and Royal Navy had been successfully using their AEW aircraft in the fighter control and strike direction roles since the late 1940s, the equivalent air forces had less luck. Historically, naval aviation operates over water, while air forces operate over the land and land, unlike the sea, has lumps and bumps – the landscape – that generate radar returns. These returns, known as clutter, created confusing images on the cathode ray tube used to view the radar 'picture' and obscured the returns from aircraft, be they hostile or friendly. Clutter did have a use, with the wartime H2S/H2X ground-mapping radars using ground returns to identify large ground features such as cities, which if near to bodies of water, stood out on the display to allow targeting.

Airborne radars such as the AN/APS-20 and its various developments (see Chapter 3) installed in the Warning Stars, Skyraiders and Gannets meant that these aircraft were pretty much restricted to over-water missions such as BARPAC and BARANT or in support of maritime operations such as Operation *Musketeer*, the Suez intervention of November 1956.

Differentiating valid target returns from clutter was a problem, and as noted above, early attempts required comparison of the readings from consecutive scans of the antenna. While this did work, it relied on skilled operators and even if such personnel were available, the radar was not sophisticated enough to handle multiple targets. As radar hardware (in the 1960s the solution *was* hardware) and signal processing developed, clutter rejection became feasible, and the first airborne moving target indicator (AMTI) was introduced on the AN/APS-82 radar carried by the E-1A Tracer.

Mention airborne early warning and the public think 'AWAC' and 'spyplane', which is how the media views any reconnaissance aircraft (probably correct in reality). If they know any 'spyplane' it's the Boeing E-3 Sentry. This Sentry, ZH101, is an RAF E-3D from No 8 Sqn and was the first delivered to the RAF in 1991. (Blue Envoy Collection)

One important role for the EC-121 Warning Star was monitoring North Vietnamese fighter activity over Indochina. Under the College Eye programme, EC-121Ds warned USAF units of enemy air operations during their air strikes. (Terry Panopalis Collection)

AMTI gained importance and much of the research and development in AEW involved AMTI and various methods to eliminate clutter and identify valid returns from aircraft. The Doppler effect was one such method as the frequency of the radar signal returned from a moving target has a phase shift that can be compared with the original signal emitted by the radar. This works fine if the radar is in a fixed position on land or a relatively slow-moving ship but in a moving aircraft whose speed relative to the target changes as the AEW aircraft manoeuvres, it is a different matter.

By the early 1970s signal processing and the associated computing capability had advanced to the extent that it was possible to provide a relatively clutter-free radar picture, and this was the catalyst for the development of a capable overland AEW platform – Sentry.

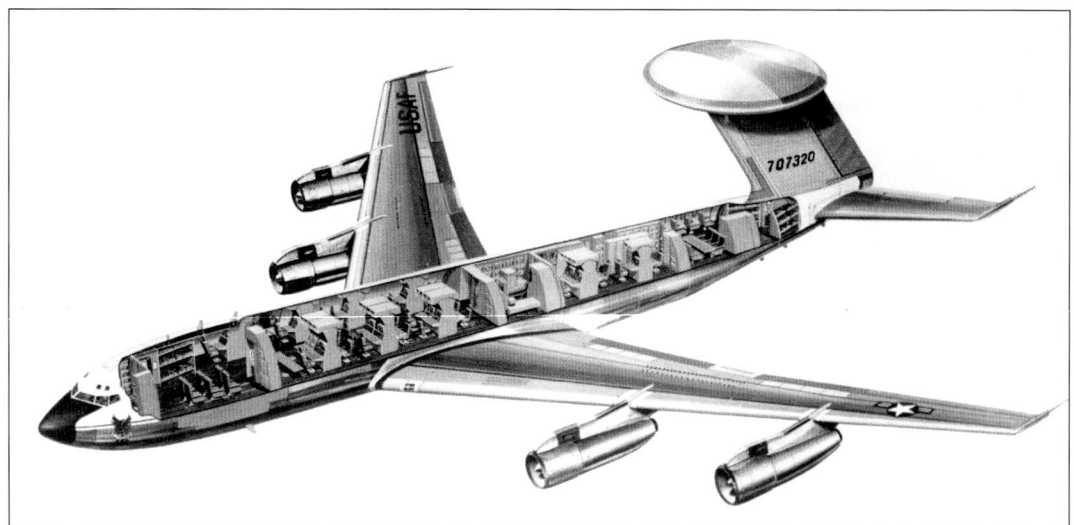

While Western analysts scoffed at the Soviet Antonov An-71 *Madcap* and its rotodome configuration, they appear to have forgotten (or didn't know) that Boeing had proposed a similar fin-mounted rotodome for its AWACS proposal. (Blue Envoy Collection)

Meanwhile, the USAF's Tactical Air Command (TAC) and Air Defense Command (ADC) had been examining what exactly they needed from an AEW aircraft with the former requiring the complete warning and control package while the latter wanted a warning system. By early 1963, TAC and ADC opted for a joint programme to develop an airborne warning and control system – AWACS. Having decided that the technology was available to provide an overland AEW capability, the USAF, in June 1965, issued requests for proposals to examine the specifics of platforms, radar and control systems. Boeing, Douglas and Lockheed all submitted proposals for the platform and Hughes, Westinghouse and Raytheon for the radar and control systems. By July 1966, Lockheed and Raytheon were dropped from the process and aircraft from Boeing and Douglas with Hughes and Westinghouse radars were admitted to the Concept Formulation Phase.

The focus then turned to the radar itself with Overland Radar Technology studies commencing in 1967, leading to a radar designation AN/APY-1 being issued to cover the AWACS radar project. By late 1971, two competing pulse-Doppler radar systems had been developed, one from Westinghouse and the other from Hughes.

By necessity this would require a large aircraft to carry the radar and computer systems and numerous airframes were proposed. Boeing's 747 was too large and a bespoke Boeing design too expensive to develop. Lockheed's modified EC-121 Warning Star, possibly based on the EC-121L (WV-2E) was used as a testbed for an AN/APS-70 radar with a rotodome, but may have been too old, and lacked development potential. The other Lockheed proposal was based on the C-141A StarLifter transport, but it was thought to suffer from severe airframe masking due to its T-tail and high wing. This left the Douglas D-989/990/991 based on the DC-8 with the variants apparently differing in their rotodome positions and whether it was based on the Jet Trader freighter or Super Sixty passenger version. The DC-8 was dismissed because it was not in service with the USAF, and instead the Boeing 707-320 airframe was selected. The argument against the DC-8 could also have been applied to the 707 as only three of the type were in service as the VC-137 VIP aircraft, although the later C-18 served in a variety of roles.

In an attempt to extend its endurance and time on station, Boeing proposed replacing the four Pratt & Whitney TF33 turbofans, rated at 21,500lbf (95.6kN) of the 707 with eight General Electric TF34 turbofans (as used on the Lockheed S-3 Viking and Fairchild A-10 Thunderbolt II) rated at 9,000lbf

One of the testbeds for the AWACS programme was EC-137D 71-1407 that had first taken to the air in spring 1972. This example tested the unsuccessful Hughes radar whereas its stablemate 71-1408 was fitted with the Westinghouse system. (Terry Panopalis Collection)

(40kN) in twin pods similar to the B-52 Stratofortress, but this was dropped after the USAF reduced the endurance requirement. Interestingly, the E-3D and F for the RAF and Armée de l'Air use the CFM-56-2A rated at 24,000lbf (110kN), which provides greater endurance than the TF34 collection.

Having selected the Boeing 707 as the platform, the first of two Brassboard test aircraft, designated EC-137D, was fitted out with the Westinghouse radar and 71-11408 took to the air on 9 February 1972. The Hughes radar made its first flight in Boeing EC-137D 71-11407 three weeks later. There then followed a fly-off between Hughes and Westinghouse to select the radar, with the latter's AN/APY-1 radar being selected. The antenna for the Westinghouse AN/APY-1 radar is mounted in a 30ft (9.1m) diameter dorsal rotodome, supported on a pair of struts. One early design study from 1967 based on the Boeing 707-320 placed a smaller rotodome at the top of a wide-chord forward-swept tail fin.

By late 1972, the Westinghouse radar and systems were deemed ready for production and the EC-137D was redesignated as the E-3A. Production started in 1975 and the first of 34 aircraft, with the official name Sentry, entered USAF service at Tinker AFB in March 1977. The Sentry has been exported to France, Saudi Arabia and the United Kingdom (after a protracted procurement process, described in Chapter 7). NATO acquired 18 Sentries, which are based at Geilenkirchen in Germany but operated under joint NATO command, with forward operating bases in Turkey, Greece, Italy and Norway.

Since the Sentry entered USAF service in 1977, it has supported US and coalition operations around the world, first seeing action during Operations *Desert Shield/Desert Storm/Granby* in 1990/91. As ever, the Sentry's radar and systems underwent regular upgrades including the Radar System Improvement Program (RSIP) from the late 1990s and the introduction of the AN/APY-2, a passive electronically scanned array radar. Thanks to these upgrades, the Sentry has remained the benchmark for AEW for 40 years, with the E-3G and its completely revised systems being the latest variant to enter service in November 2015, with an electronic support measures (ESM) capability that took the Sentry's performance beyond just AEW.

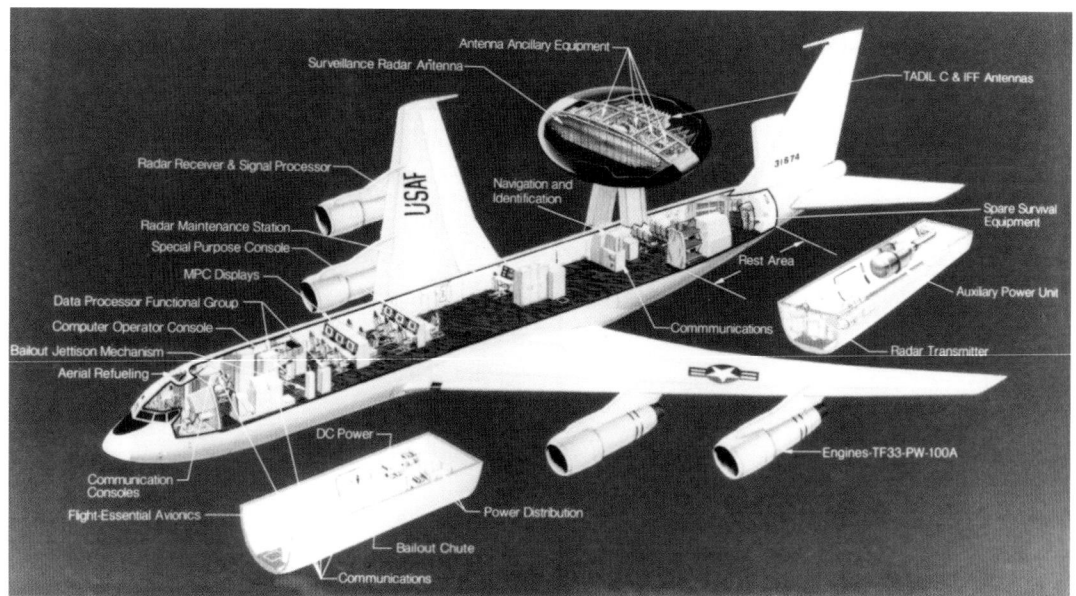

When the EC-137 became the E-3A Sentry, the USAF knew the platform would be a success. This cutaway drawing shows the internal layout and the workstations for the various operators. (Blue Envoy Collection)

When it entered USAF service in March 1977, the Sentry was paired with the McDonnell Douglas F-4E Phantom. E-3A Sentry 61615 is accompanied by Phantoms 66330 and 66382. (Blue Envoy Collection)

NATO's Sentries, such as 11407, seen here on a predelivery flight, are based at NATO Air Base Geilenkirchen in Germany and operate with Luxemburg registrations. They are essentially the same as the USAF's Sentries and are crewed by personnel from 17 of the NATO members. (Blue Envoy Collection)

Relieving the Sentry

What can follow a successful platform such as the Sentry? Hawkeye has been replaced by a Hawkeye, but despite a few attempts, no replacement had been formally identified until 2022. Boeing, Northrop Grumman and Raytheon had proposed the E-10, also known as the Multi-Sensor Command and Control Aircraft (MC2A) in 2003. Derived from the Boeing 767-400ER airliner, the E-10 was intended as a replacement for the E-3 Sentry, RC-135 Rivet Joint, E-8 Joint Surveillance Target Attack Radar System (JSTARS) battlefield management platform and the E-4B command post. Initially, all three roles were to be combined in a single airframe, but the probability of interference between the radars, as well as the power requirements, soon brought an end to that idea.

In the three phases or 'Spirals' of E-10 development, so named for their increasing capability, Spiral 1 was to augment (or replace, given its age) the E-8 JSTARS, while Spiral 3 was a replacement for the RC-135 Rivet Joint series. The variant to replace the Sentry was in Spiral 2 and was intended to use the same Multi-Role Electronically Scanned Array (MESA) used on the E-7. This was cancelled with no successor system specified. Artists' impressions of the original E-10 showed it with the MESA radar just forward of the tailfin, in the style of the E-7 Wedgetail, with the 'canoe' for the AN/APY-7 side-looking airborne radar (SLAR) from the JSTARS under the forward fuselage.

The Japanese Air Self-Defense Force (JASDF) sought the E-3 Sentry in the late 1970s following the defection of a Soviet Air Force MiG-25 *Foxbat* to Japan in September 1976. Boeing was fully committed to production of Sentries for the USAF, so the JASDF opted for the Hawkeye. In 1991, the JASDF again requested the Sentry to replace/supplement the Hawkeye but by then the Boeing 707 was long out of production. The solution was to take the AN/APY-2 radar and systems used on Sentry and install them

With the Boeing 707 and E-3 Sentry long gone from the production lines, the Japanese Air Self Defence Force opted for installing the Sentry's systems in the Boeing 767, producing the E-767. A JASDF E-767, 84-3504, cuts a dash over Honshū, showing off its rotodome and framing Mt Fuji under its starboard wing. (JASDF via Wiki Commons)

Showing its MESA antenna, a RAAF Wedgetail A30-002 of No 2 Sqn RAAF takes off on a surveillance mission. No 2 Sqn operates six Wedgetails from RAAF Williamtown, near Newcastle, New South Wales. A permanent detachment is based at RAAF Tindal, Northern Territory. (Cpl Craig Barrett, RAAF)

on a Boeing 767-200ER to become the E-767. Japan purchased four examples of what is effectively the AWACS equipment installed in a 767.

Since then, Boeing has, at the behest of the Royal Australian Air Force (RAAF), developed the E-7, known to the Australians as 'Wedgetail', named for the largest eagle in Australia. The E-7 has been proposed, and adopted, as a USAF Sentry successor and when the second largest Sentry operator, NATO, began to look at replacing the Sentry, it examined the E-7 and the SAAB GlobalEye. At the time of writing, in March 2023, no decision had been made.,

Sentry will always be viewed as the AEW system that epitomised the role. The popular press usually referred to it as an 'Awac' as if AWACS was plural and invariably describe it as a 'spy plane'. Whatever name is applied, the Sentry was for almost half a century the AEW&C system of choice for Western air forces. For much of those five decades it had no competition, but not without others trying.

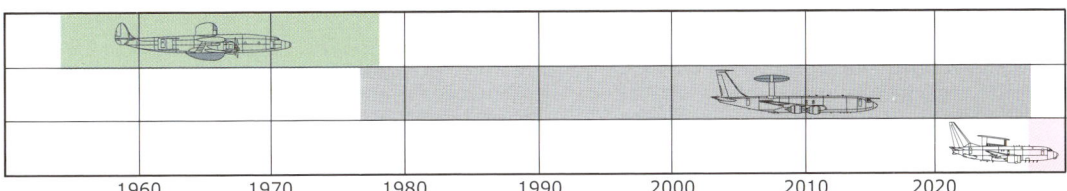

Surprisingly, given its reliance on force multiplier aircraft, the USAF has only fielded two AEW aircraft since World War Two. Perhaps they selected well. (Author)

Chapter 6

UK AEW – The Baggers

'…the Navy are drawn to think of AEW as a role specifically for the defence of the Fleet'. Deputy Commander-in-Chief at Strike Command, Air Marshal Sir Peter Bairsto, 1981

Having taken the lead in AEW during World War Two, the British promptly lost it in the postwar years. As noted above, operating radars such as the AN/APS-20 over land was problematic so the RAF opted to wait for the overland capability to become available. At one point in the 1950s a suggestion was put forward, possibly a Staff College project, to fit a ventral radar in the style of the Warning Star to the Avro Vulcan, but this did not proceed as the Vulcans were needed for carrying the deterrent. Until the 1970s, it was the Royal Navy that operated AEW aircraft in Britain's armed forces, initially with Douglas AD-4W Skyraiders and later, Fairey Gannets, from its carriers. On paying off HMS *Ark Royal* in 1978, the Royal Navy lost its AEW capability. Four years later and following a disaster in the South Atlantic, AEW was back in the Fleet Air Arm (FAA).

The RAF gained its first truly operational AEW squadron in 1972, when the Avro Shackleton AEW2 entered service. Fitted with hand-me-down AN/APS-20 sets, they operated in the GIUK Gap until replaced, after a long procurement process often described as a disaster, by the E-3 Sentry. It is an interesting, if convoluted, story.

Guarding the Fleet

Had World War Two continued into 1946, the Fleet Air Arm would have been operating alongside the US Navy during the invasion of Japan. Like the Americans, the British intended to use AEW aircraft for fighter control against the Kamikaze and strike direction in support of the landings of Dominion, United Kingdom and Empire (DUKE) forces on the Japanese Home Islands. For this, the Admiralty planned

Seen head on, the Gannet AEW3 XJ440 looks rather stylish, certainly compared with its portly anti-submarine siblings. The Gannet was powered by an Armstrong Siddeley Double-Mamba engine driving contrarotating propellers. Each Mamba drove one of the propellers, so one engine could be shut down in flight to extend endurance. (Terry Panopalis Collection)

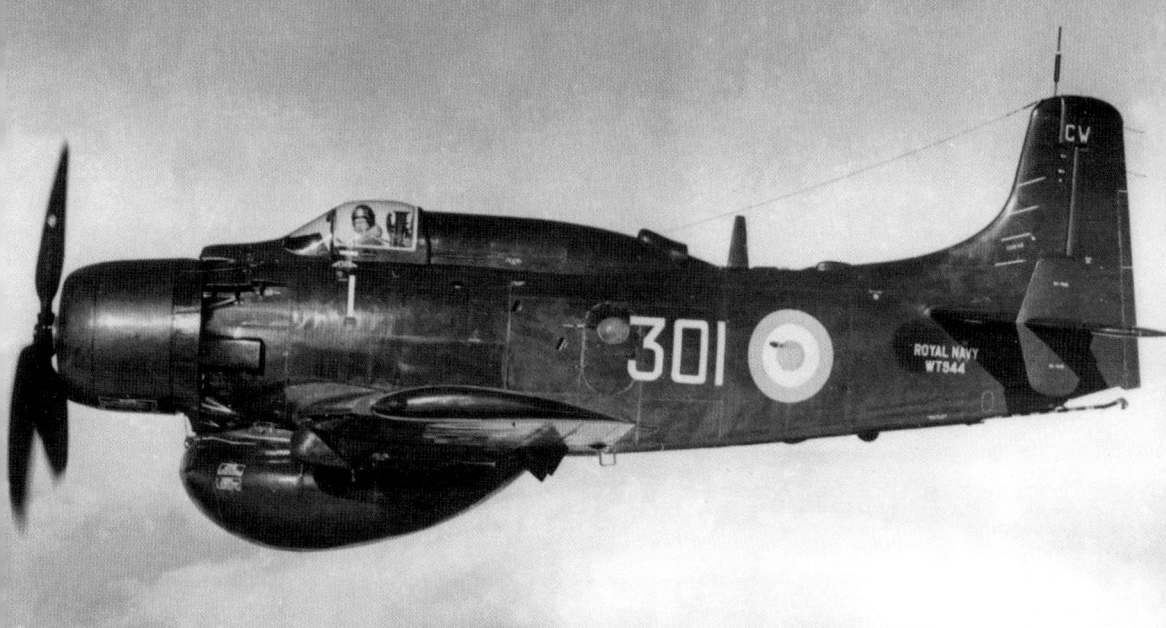

Douglas Skyraider AEW1s served on Royal Navy carriers throughout the 1950s providing valuable experience for future operations with Gannet. This view of WT844 shows the size of the radome as well as, forward of the '301' marking, the entrance to the rear cabin where the operators worked. (Blue Envoy Collection)

to fit the AN/APS-20 radar in the Fairey Spearfish, a large single-engined multirole aircraft in the same class as the Douglas Skyraider.

When the war against Japan abruptly ended in August 1945, the need for the AEW Spearfish disappeared but not for long. The FAA again operated with the US Navy during the Korean War and as part of the expansion of armed forces that the conflict prompted, it acquired 50 US Navy surplus Skyraiders in 1951 under the Military Assistance Program (MAP). These were operated as the Skyraider AEW1 in the early warning, air defence co-ordination and strike direction roles with each carrier equipped with a flight of four aircraft from 849 Naval Air Squadron (NAS) with 778 NAS handling training for the first year of service. The Skyraider AEW1 took part in Operation *Musketeer* during the Suez Crisis of November 1956 with aircraft flying from HMS *Eagle* and HMS *Albion*. The type was very successful and was in frontline service until 1962, when the last of the Skyraiders was withdrawn.

In the late 1950s, the Admiralty took the decision to banish gasoline from its ships and make all aircraft gas turbine-powered, fuelled with less flammable kerosene. This prompted the retirement of the piston-engined helicopters and aircraft such as the Skyraider AEW1 fleet, and by 1962 they were gone,

From 1951, the Royal Navy's carriers were equipped with the Douglas Skyraider AEW1. They were probably the last piston-engined fixed wing aircraft to operate from the Navy's carriers. Interestingly, it is the Westland Dragonfly that has attracted the crowd on deck. (Blue Envoy Collection)

Deck crew disconnect the towbar from Skyraider AEW1 WV180 prior to take off. The pilot's canopy is open to improve the chance of escaping should the aircraft ditch on take-off. The two crew in the rear cabin had no such assistance. (Blue Envoy Collection)

with the Skyraiders replaced by an AEW variant of the Fairey Gannet anti-submarine warfare (ASW) type. Such was the redesign work on the ASW Gannet's fuselage, it was essentially a new aircraft that was originally to be called Albatross, but since the ASW Gannets were being replaced in that role by helicopters, the Gannet name was retained.

Also retained was the AN/APS-20F radar from the Skyraiders, and these were installed under the Gannet's fuselage. As noted above, the fuselage was pretty much a new design as the pot-bellied original lacked ground clearance for the radome. The Armstrong Siddeley Double Mamba turboprops were fitted with shorter jet pipes, neatly nestled between the wing root and radome. The Gannet AEW3 also carried the AN/ART-28 Bellhop that transmitted the radar picture to the aircraft carrier's control centre, known at the time as the Aircraft Direction Room.

The first of 44 Gannet AEW3s took to the air in August 1958 and after trials and training, the type entered operational service with 849 NAS in January 1960. The squadron was split into five Flights (one of which was a headquarters unit) with four aircraft, plus a Gannet COD4 variant, per flight on each carrier. The Gannet served until HMS *Ark Royal*, the last of the Royal Navy's conventional carriers, was

By 1960, the moratorium on using gasoline on Her Majesty's warships, meant the Skyraiders had been replaced by the Fairey Gannet AEW3. Gannets provided two-engine safety and modernised systems but relied on the AN/APS-20 radar from the Skyraiders. Two Gannet AEW3s, XL450 042R and XL471 043R, are readied for take-off from HMS *Ark Royal* in March 1978. (Terry Panopalis Collection)

The size of the Fairey Gannet AEW3, particularly the ventral radome, is obvious from the deck crewmen manhandling the catapult strop attached to XL450 as it is readied for catapult launch from HMS *Ark Royal* in March 1978. (Terry Panopalis Collection)

paid off in 1978 and a Fairey Gannet AEW3 was the last FAA aircraft to land on a conventional aircraft carrier of the Royal Navy. In most navies, AEW aircraft were usually first to launch and last to land, to provide surveillance for operations.

The Baggers

Four years after paying off HMS *Ark Royal* and the departure of the Royal Navy's AEW capability, a situation arose in the South Atlantic. Argentina had occupied the Falkland Islands and a British task force was despatched to recover them. In the order of battle of Argentine Naval Aviation were five Dassault Super Étendards, armed with the Aerospatiale AM39 Exocet anti-ship missiles, which could be launched from low altitude and thus below the radar horizon of the Royal Navy's anti-aircraft vessels. Interestingly, target identification and direction of the Super Étendards was carried out by Argentine Naval Aviation Lockheed SP-2H Neptunes using the AN/APS-20 radar.

Ships hit by anti-ship missiles included HMS *Sheffield*, which was armed with missiles designed to tackle high altitude Soviet bombers such as the Tupolev Tu-22M *Backfire*. *Sheffield* was struck by an Exocet and sunk; the container ship SS *Atlantic Conveyor* was struck by two Exocets, and was so heavily damaged it sunk while under tow. One consequence of the loss of SS *Atlantic Conveyor* was the destruction of six Westland Wessexes, three Boeing-Vertol Chinooks, a Westland Lynx, most of the Pierced Steel Planking to build runways on the islands and invaluable stores. The loss of the

Chinooks alone hampered the land war, as the troops had to walk across East Falkland and all stores had to be carried across boggy terrain rather than airlifted.

The lack of AEW cover for the fleet prompted consternation in the Ministry of Defence (MoD). Early warning of air attack was required, and the only feasible method was radar picket ships, which made them vulnerable to air attack. One proposal involved using the sonobuoys dropped by Nimrods to 'listen' for aircraft noise and transmit their signals either to warships or the Nimrods. This was an established practice as Soviet *Bear*s and other turboprop maritime patrol aircraft could be detected by sonobuoys. Trials in the English Channel proved that the sonobuoys were not sensitive enough, but it was hoped that the Army could supply more sensitive microphones, possibly the same ones used for gun location by the Royal Artillery. Perhaps low-flying strike aircraft lack the sonar signature of a Tupolev Tu-95 *Bear*. Another factor against the sonobuoy idea was that to set a line of sonobuoys west of the task force would require Nimrods fitted with air-to-air refuelling (AAR) probes and a number of Victor K2 tankers to support the Nimrods. At the time of this request, the former didn't yet exist, and the latter were fully stretched so the proposal was dropped.

A more successful proposal saw the resurrection of a Westland design study from the late 1970s, which itself was an updated study from 1966. This early work involved fitting a Westland Sea King HAS1 with an AEW radar that could either be mounted under the nose in a large radome or as a larger rotating antenna that could be retracted into a ventral recess. At the time this elicited little interest from the Admiralty, as

Post-Falklands, the Sea King AEW2 was embarked on the *Illustrious*-class aircraft carriers. Sea King XV671, seen here with HMS *Illustrious*, underwent many upgrades, ending its days as an Airborne Surveillance and Control (ASaC)7. (Blue Envoy Collection)

At sea, the AEW/interceptor team for the Royal Navy's Fleet Air Arm was the Sea Harrier FRS1 and Sea King AEW2. This pair are over HMS *Illustrious* in the mid-1980s before the ship underwent a major refit that removed the forward Sea Dart SAM launcher and magazine. (Blue Envoy Collection)

the RAF was to provide AEW cover to the fleet in the eastern North Atlantic, but in the light of events in the Falklands the Admiralty became very interested and the dust was blown off the design study.

The 1982 solution also used the Sea King ASW machine but this time it carried a modified Thorn-EMI Searchwater radar (as used on the new Nimrods being upgraded to MR2 standard) housed in an inflatable Kevlar radome on the starboard side of the fuselage. The ASW kit was stripped out and replaced with the radar systems and two operator panels. To provide an unrestricted 360° view, the radome was mounted on an assembly that allowed the radome to be positioned clear of the lower fuselage but rotated upwards and rearwards through 90° for take-off and landing. Its saggy appearance, when stowed and deflated, led to the AEW Sea Kings being known as 'Baggers'. The prototype Sea King HAS2(AEW)s were operating with D Flight 824NAS from HMS *Illustrious* within 11 weeks of the go-ahead and the fully developed production version, the Sea King AEW2, entered service in 1985.

The AEW variants of the Sea King underwent regular upgrades, including the Searchwater SW2000AEW radar and Cerberus mission systems that culminated in the AEW7, which was subsequently redesignated as the Airborne Surveillance and Control (ASaC)7 to reflect its much-enhanced capability that could track 400 targets and provide over-the-horizon targeting for missiles as well as a surface picture for the fleet. The Admiralty was very pleased with its Sea King AEWs and more than happy with the ASaC7s and Cerberus. The Sea King could provide commanders with an overall view of air traffic and the marine and

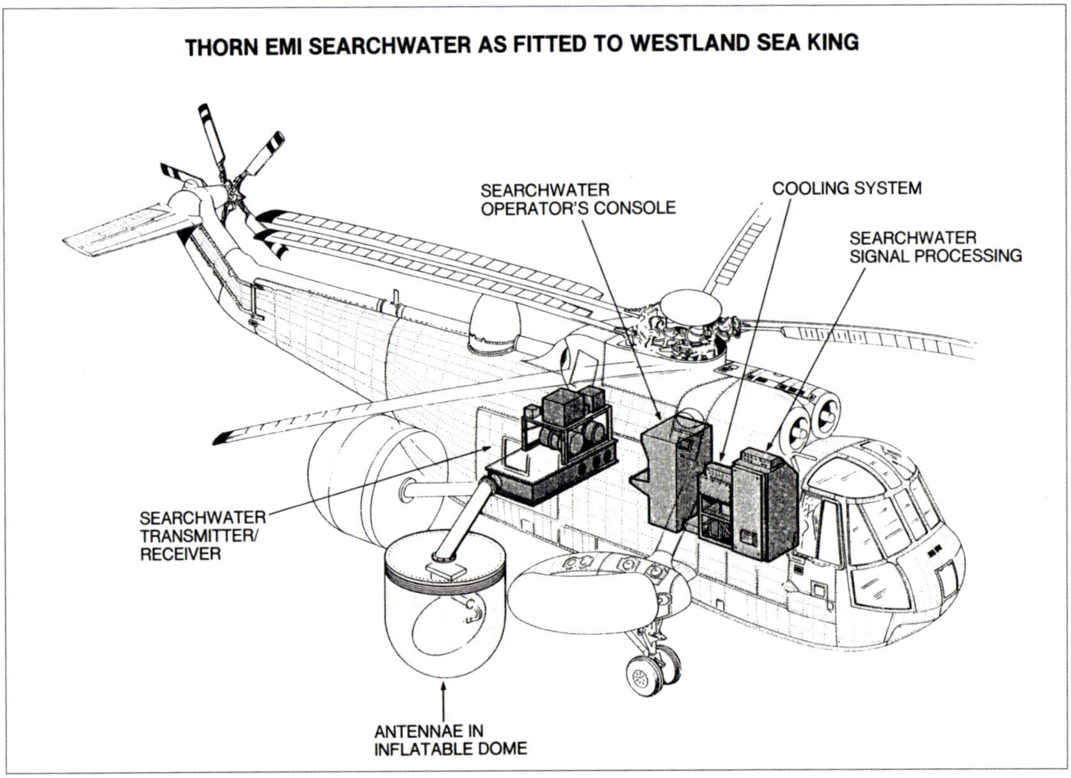

THORN EMI SEARCHWATER AS FITTED TO WESTLAND SEA KING

A cutaway diagram illustrating of the main components and workstations for the Searchwater radar of the Sea King AEW2. (Blue Envoy Collection)

This 'bagger' has its Searchwater AEW radar deployed and is on patrol. The radar was derived from the air-to-surface vessel radar used on the Nimrod MR2. When first discussed as an emergency AEW platform, the RAF complained that it would lose two sets from the Nimrod upgrade programme. The Admiralty won the day. (Blue Envoy Collection)

land situations. In effect the ASaC7 combined its AEW role with a surveillance capability almost on a par with the RAF's Raytheon Sentinel R1 or the USAF's Boeing E-8 JSTARS in a compact, ship-borne platform.

The Fleet Air Arm's ASaC7 Sea Kings were, like the ASW and commando support fleet, replaced by the AW101 Merlin, with the last AEW Sea King retired in 2018. The AEW kit for the Merlin was intended to be modular and able to be fitted to any of the standard ASW Merlin HM2s in the fleet. Called Crowsnest, the palletised system retains the Cerberus mission systems and Searchwater radar, with the antenna in a

Above: The ultimate variant of the Sea King AEW was the Westland Sea King ASaC7. This example, with its radome deflated and folded, was spotted on the flight deck of HMS *Ark Royal* during a visit to North Shields in 2010. (Kirsten Black)

Right: The replacement for the Sea King ASaC7 was Project Crowsnest, which involved an upgraded Searchwater radar mission system installed on a pallet that could be installed on the AgustaWestland AW101 Merlin HM2. (MoD/Open Government Licence)

retractable, inflatable radome that now swings upwards for take-off and landing, fitted on the port side of the cabin. Crowsnest Merlins were first deployed aboard HMS *Queen Elizabeth* in 2021 on that year's Carrier Strike Group deployment to the Far East. The latest versions of Crowsnest include a much-enhanced overland performance and better communications with the RAF and FAA Lockheed F-35 Lightnings.

All in all, the Royal Navy and Fleet Air Arm has applied the AEW technology and equipment it fielded with great success. Unfortunately, in their time of need, the capability was not available. The day that armed forces around the world woke up to the fact that an airborne early warning system was a necessity, not a luxury, was arguably 4 May 1982. Some services had known this for years but had been stymied at every turn. This was the case with the Royal Air Force.

Unlike their predecessors, the 'bag' on the Merlin HM2 Crowsnest swings upward through 90° when not in use. This example is undergoing maintenance and has the 'bag' deflated. (MoD/Open Government Licence)

In May 1982, the Royal Navy learned just how critical AEW was to naval operations. The UK Ministry of Defence's (MoD's) plans to use land-based AEW platforms to protect the fleet fell flat in the vastness of the South Atlantic. (Author)

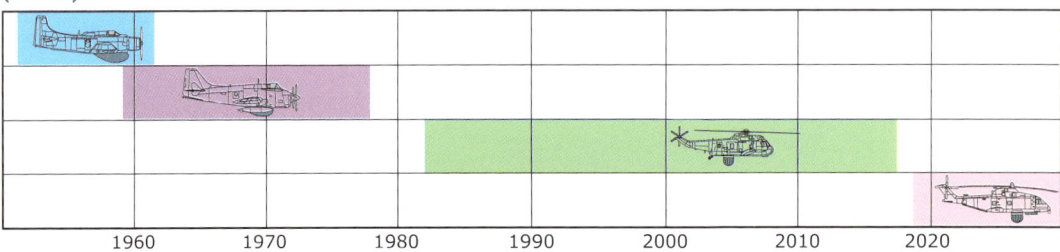

Chapter 7

Overland But All At Sea – The RAF and AEW

'I did not spend three hours flying over the North Sea fiddling with a system in Nimrod that did not work. The question is how well it works against the stark demand of Air Staff Requirement [ASR] 400'.
The Rt Hon George Younger, Secretary of State for Defence, 18 December 1986.

While the Royal Navy has a long and, aside from May 1982, comparatively trouble-free relationship with AEW, the same cannot be said for the RAF. The pioneers of AEW did not field an operational AEW type until 1972, mainly because the radars of the era were unsuited to operations over land due to clutter, making detection and tracking of targets problematic. Ironically, the aircraft that did enter service, the Shackleton AEW2, used the same radar, the AN/APS-20, that the RAF had used for trials in 1948 when it was deemed no better than the ASV 13, and in 1952 it was judged too difficult to operate!

The first of these trials, Operation *Haddock* in 1948, as described in Chapter 3, assessed the US Navy's PB-1W. The *Vanguard* trials four years later involved a flight of four RAF Coastal Command Lockheed Neptune MR1s lent to Fighter Command (as 1453 Flight, a name that has been used repeatedly for special purposes since 1940) to assess the practicality of AEW and the effectiveness of the AN/APS-20 radar. The trials went well, with the radar capable of picking up a Canberra flying at 300ft (91m) over the sea at a distance of 75 miles (150km). While this was highly satisfactory, such performance was only

By the time the Nimrod AEW3s were cancelled they were fitted with refuelling probes (in 1978, such things were deemed unnecessary, but that changed in 1982) and finished in a rather handsome hemp scheme. Nimrod AEW3 XV263, banking away on a photographic sortie. (Blue Envoy Collection)

The RAF continued its wartime interest in AEW with Operation *Haddock*, which pitted US Navy PB-1W Fortresses against Coastal Command Warwicks. In a subsequent 1955 AEW trial, three Coastal Command Neptune MR1s were lent to Fighter Command as 1453 (Vanguard) Flight. While successful, scaling it up would have been expensive. Neptune MR1 WX505 is operating with one engine during a photographic sortie in the early 1950s. (Blue Envoy Collection)

possible if the radar sets were 'tweaked' and the main criticism was that the radars were delicate and required constant maintenance.

The report on *Vanguard* recommended a larger aircraft carrying a larger radar and that the existing system worked best when the information was passed to a ground station. Unsurprising, as that was the original modus operandi of the AN/APS-20 Cadillac system from 1945 and may be the origin of the Vulcan AEW proposal.

From 1952, aside from basic research, the Royal Navy carried the torch for AEW operations in the UK, but in 1962 the Air Staff and Admiralty issued a joint requirement, NASR6166, for an AEW type for both services. This was heavily weighted towards the Navy's requirement for a carrier-borne machine resulting in the Blackburn P.139, which the Air Staff considered too small and thus unsuitable for the RAF. It was the cancellation of the Royal Navy's new CVA carriers that ultimately led to NASR6166's downfall in February 1966 but another factor that finally stymied development for the RAF was the lack of a radar with overland capability.

Subsequently, after a re-examination of the RAF's needs (the writing had been on the wall for the aircraft carriers since mid-1965), ASR387 was issued in April 1966. It was clear to the Air Staff that the new AEW aircraft would take time to develop so a stopgap pending the arrival in service of an AEW type to meet ASR387 (and subsequently ASR400) was required. In 1970, ASR394 was issued, covering the fitting of the AN/APS-20F radars from the FAA's Gannets (previously fitted to Skyraiders) on a land-based platform. The radar's performance was enhanced by the addition of an Elliott Brothers AMTI system and since this worked best on a slow-flying aircraft, the radar was fitted to the Shackleton MR2, becoming the Shackleton AEW2.

The MR2 variant, with its anachronistic tail-dragger undercarriage, was selected because the more modern Shackleton MR3s, complete with modern tricycle undercarriage, sound insulation and a functional galley, had limited fatigue life. This was due to the MR3 being fitted with Armstrong Siddeley Viper 203 turbojets in the outer engine nacelles. These were intended to reduce the load on the

Changing of the guard. Two AEW aircraft that failed to leave the drawing board were the 'Big Picture' Stratofreighter and Blackburn's P.139. Aimed at NASR6166, the P.139 was too small for the RAF and by the time it would have entered service, the Royal Navy would have no carriers. (Adrian Mann)

The Growler reborn. Long after its maritime patrol-roled forebears had disappeared from squadron service, the Shackleton AEW2 filled a gap in the RAF's order of battle. That gap was to last much longer than the Air Staff ever imagined. (Woodford Collection)

Rolls-Royce Griffon and allow a heavier all-up weight. Unfortunately using the Vipers put additional strain on the airframe.

On entering service with No 8 Sqn at Kinloss in September 1972, they were billed as a temporary measure, required to provide AEW cover for the fleet in the eastern North Atlantic until the new AEW type to meet ASR387 arrived. In this role they would mainly operate over the sea, where the AN/APS-20 radar would work as required. The squadron moved to Lossiemouth in August 1973 and remained there until retirement in 1991.

The 12 Shackleton AEW2s were named after characters from the TV series *The Magic Roundabout* (such as Dougal, Florence, Zebedee and ironically, Mr Rusty) and *The Herbs* (Parsley, PC Knapweed, Dill). The 'interim' Shackletons growled around northeast Scotland for a lot longer than ever imagined.

Very much cutting-edge, ASR 387 called for a new type of radar. This was the frequency modulated interrupted continuous wave (FMICW) radar (see Appendix 2) that offered the overland capability required by the Air Staff. This radar was being developed by the Radar Research Establishment (RRE) and what would soon become Marconi-Elliott Avionics. This radar was to be installed on a Hawker Siddeley Andover and since FMICW and propellers were incompatible, the Andover was to be powered by two Rolls-Royce RB.203 Trent turbofans rated at 9,980lbf (44.4kN). This was the second iteration of

Left: The hand-me-down radars of Skyraider, Gannet and Shackleton are preserved in many museums around the UK. This AN/APS-20 antenna, recovered from a Shackleton AEW2 is displayed in its transport frame at the Midlands Air Museum at Coventry Airport. (Author)

Below: Not a dorsal-mounted Phantom but the defenders of the GIUK Gap in formation. The No 23 Sqn Phantom FGR2 XV406 has flaps deployed and undercarriage lowered to hold station with No 8 Sqn Shackleton AEW2 WL757, making maximum noise. (Terry Panopalis Collection)

the name for a Rolls-Royce engine, the first was the RB.50 turboprop of 1944 while the latest is the RB.211 derivative rated at 97,000lbf (431kN) in its Trent XWB variant. The other novel feature of the Andover AEW was that it featured the scanners in a fore-and-aft configuration with an antenna in the nose and one in the tail, synchronised to provide 360° coverage, which became known as the fore-and-aft scanning system (FASS).

A number of design studies for ASR387 appeared, mounting the radar on any aircraft that could lift the kit, including the Lockheed Hercules, Breguet Atlantique and 'standard' Andovers. Some of the most interesting studies were based on the Vickers VC10 and BAC One-Eleven with a retractable spherical radome on a ventral mounting, FASS and rotodomes. BAC Bristol pitched Britannia Early Warning Airborne Radar Equipment (BEWARE) comprising a Britannia transport with the Hawkeye's AN/APS-120 radar. The BAC One-Eleven was deemed too small and lacked endurance while the VC10 was too big and expensive. BEWARE didn't use the new radar and lacked a suitable power supply to run the AN/APS-120. Another type proposed for ASR387 was the Hawker Siddeley Andover, in a variety of configurations; FASS, dorsal rotodome and retractable ventral 'kettle drum'. This proposal, converted to use four de Havilland Gnome turboprops rather than Rolls-Royce Darts was the preferred option, but all that was about to change because lurking in the background were the American Overland Radar Technology studies that would lead to Sentry.

As noted in Chapter 5, the Americans had pretty much solved the overland conundrum by using pulse-Doppler and sophisticated computer power in a Boeing 707 rather than FMICW in an Andover and as the work on ASR387 progressed it became apparent that the British needed to rethink their options. In 1963, FMICW, or rather its reduced dependence on signal processing, had been a sound choice but by the end of the decade computers had become smaller and more powerful. In August 1970, the Working Party on Airborne Radar recommended that the work on FMICW be stopped and a pulse-Doppler radar adopted. Unfortunately, Marconi-Elliott Avionics had just delivered to the RRE a test article of the FMICW radar that *Flight International* described as having 'performed satisfactorily'. Despite such encouraging results, development effort transferred to a pulse-Doppler system and its attendant computers, which would not fit in an Andover, nor would that type have sufficient electrical power.

By the end of the 1970s and with the UK's withdrawal from East of Suez, ASR 387 was suffering from 'mission creep' and was garnering additional roles, such as maritime surveillance. In the light of this and after several revisions, it was cancelled in favour of a much more demanding requirement, ASR400, issued in 1972. This placed more emphasis on overland capability as it was also required to operate over NATO's Central Front, possibly as part of a NATO AEW force that would play a key role in the flexible response policy that had been adopted by the Western Alliance and France.

A variety of airframes were examined for ASR400. Plessey, Racal and Ferranti pitched a re-engined Boeing 707 (essentially a Sentry with British kit), Lockheed a P-3 Orion with Hawkeye's AN/APS-145 radar, Grumman pitched the E-2 Hawkeye and a Nimrod with a dorsal AN/APS-145 that invariably became known as 'Hawkrod'.

Orion AEW, Hawkeye and Hawkrod were dismissed due to fears that the AN/APS-145 radar might interfere with civilian radios while Sentry, despite the Air Staff's desires, was dropped as too expensive

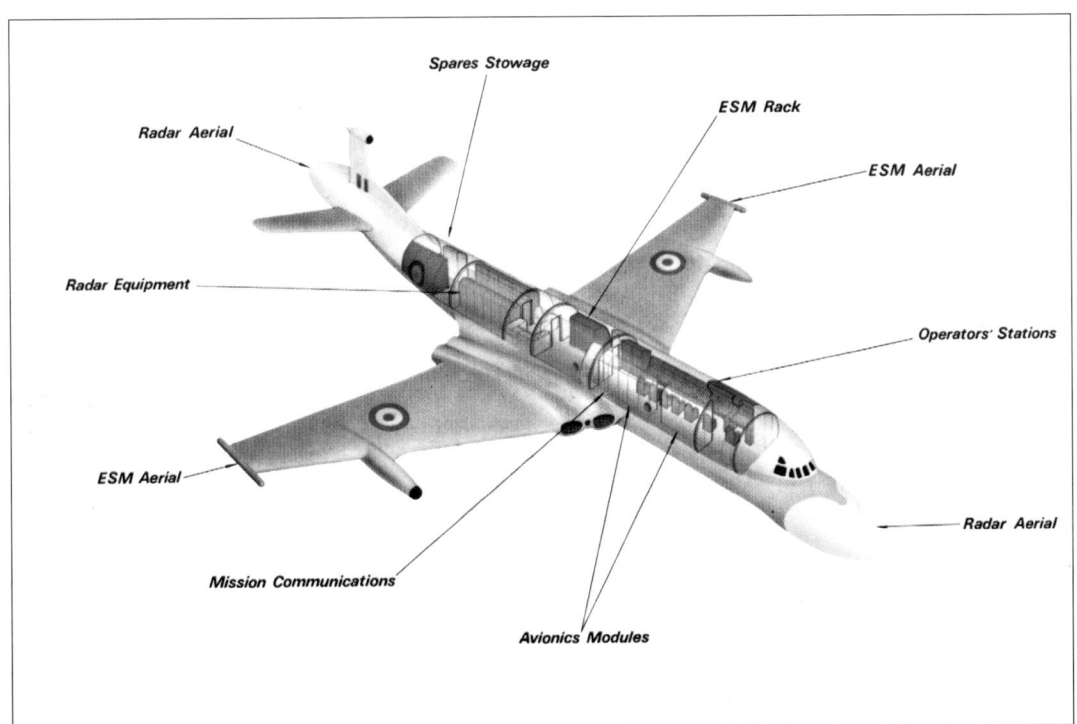

The various workstations and sensors of the Nimrod AEW are laid out in this cutaway diagram of the Nimrod in the early days of its development. The final machine was much more complex. (Blue Envoy Collection)

and the AN/APY-1/2 radar interfered with Blindfire radar used by the Rapier SAMs of the Army and the RAF Regiment. The MOD, holders of the purse strings, was adamant that there should be a cheaper, British solution to the long-running AEW question.

As luck would have it, the withdrawal of British forces from the Mediterranean freed up several surplus Nimrods. These were faster and higher-flying than the Andovers and would be ideal for conversion to AEW platforms and thus the Nimrod AEW3 was born. The whole situation was further compounded by NATO prevaricating on its selection of an AEW platform with the choice now being between the Nimrod AEW and the E-3 Sentry. The British MOD was likely to adopt whatever type NATO opted for, hoping for a large order for Nimrod from NATO. However, Britain's need for an AEW platform fit for the 1980s and beyond was much more immediate and in the face of indecision, the British government took the plunge and funded Nimrod AEW.

The Nimrods would carry a Marconi-Elliott pulse-Doppler radar with a pair of inverse Cassegrain antennas, one mounted in the nose, the other in the tail in what is called a fore-and-aft scanner system (FASS). In reality, the Nimrod was a bit too small for the pulse-Doppler radar, but the development of computing was bringing increased power and capability and reducing in size. Computers could only get smaller.

To test the system, a de Havilland Comet 4C XW626 was modified to carry a test system, with a single antenna and its radome grafted onto the nose. The Comet AEW took to the air in March 1977, while Nimrod AEW development continued with the first converted Nimrod AEW3 airframe flying in July 1980 and the first 'production' example taking to the air in March 1983. The first protype was to test flight characteristics, which were described as better than the maritime patrol versions, while the second prototype was fitted out with what Marconi Avionics called Mission Systems Avionics (MSA) namely the radar and computers.

It soon became evident that all was not well with the Nimrod AEW programme and that Marconi might just be out of their depth. The subsequent events and their outcomes are extremely difficult to relate objectively, and all the participants have their own versions of events. Suffice to say the blame was spread less than equally. Many of the stories associated with Nimrod AEW3 are difficult to substantiate and all are rather partisan.

One reason for the delay on the decision to proceed with the Nimrod AEW project was the lack of clarity on the NATO AEW force. The UK, with a pressing need for a Shackleton replacement, lost patience and ordered Nimrod. The European members of NATO opted for the Sentry. Seen on a pre-delivery flight, E-3A Sentry 90442, became one of the first to enter service with the NATO E-3A Component. (Blue Envoy Collection)

Trials of the Marconi MSA in Comet XM626 showed that the system was feasible. Based on these trials three Nimrod MR1 airframes were earmarked for conversion to the full FASS configuration as preproduction machines for trials. (Blue Envoy Collection)

The investment was billed as the biggest waste of taxpayers' money ever (that was in 1986, before Chinook HC3, Nimrod MRA4 or the *Astute*-class submarine, Ajax armoured fighting vehicle and Voyager tanker.) The Nimrod AEW3 was derided in the press for overheating in the sun and for tracking the Ford Sierra RS Cosworths of Aberdeen and tracking the Ferrari Testarossas of Edinburgh as they drove around the bypass. All great stories have an element of truth and both tales were essentially accurate. The former happened while the radar was being operated on the ground as the fuel acted as a heat sink for the computers but, lacking the airflow that passed over the wing in flight, the fuel heated up in the sun. The latter was due to the Air Staff's requirement for detection of slow-moving helicopters and ships to provide a surface picture to the fleet.

These surface returns produced a myriad of 'targets' which the computers struggled to keep tabs on and eventually, overloaded, the computers threw in the towel and stopped working. The problem would be solved by upgrading the computer from the GEC 4080 to the 4190F with higher capacity and replacing the inverse Cassegrain antennas with offset parabolic designs. The other improvements were software related with the addition of a 'vehicle correlator' to remove road vehicles from the tracking systems.

From Avenger to Nimrod. Oddly enough, as the problems with the Marconi MSA mounted, the Nimrod airframes were airborne and were considered to handle better than the maritime patrol variants. At one point, frustrated by lack of progress on the radar, the MoD suggested replacing the MSA with the AN/APS-20 sets from the Shackleton, two sets per Nimrod! Quite apt as airframe and radar dated from the 1940s. Avro Shackleton AEW2 WR960 and BAe Nimrod AEW3 XZ285 fly in formation over the North Sea. (Blue Envoy Collection)

Above left: Looking forward in the Nimrod AEW3. Compare this image with that of the E-3 Sentry on page 50 While the Nimrod was cramped, the Sentry was spacious. However, within 20 years, aircraft smaller than Nimrod were delivering similar capabilities. (Blue Envoy Collection)

Above right: It was the future – Nimrod AEW3 directing Tornado F2s onto Soviet *Bear* and *Backfire* bombers in the Greenland Iceland UK Gap. The Air Staff had high hopes for the Nimrod/Tornado team, but Nimrod was scrapped and the Tornado F2, beset with radar problems, evolved into the F3, which did exactly what it was supposed to. BAe Nimrod AEW3 XZ286 and Panavia Tornado F2 ADV prototype ZA267 were displayed at Farnborough in the early 1980s. (Blue Envoy Collection)

The ongoing problems prompted late nights at Marconi's Borehamwood works and by late 1986 Marconi claimed that it had solved the problems. Unfortunately for Marconi, the MOD had had enough, and as Marconi were delivering the revised MSA in late 1986, a complete review of the programme was launched.

The same types from the original ASR400 process were re-examined, including a Hawkrod that combined the Nimrod AEW3 airframe, minus the nose radome, with the AN/APS-145 rotodome from Hawkeye. If the AEW3 was considered ugly, the 1986 Hawkrod redefined ugliness in aircraft. Rank

With the demise of the Nimrod AEW programme, one of the many types proposed for ASR400 was the AEW Defender. This comprised a BN-2T-4 Defender fitted with a radar. Two variants were built; one, G-TEMI, with Thorn-EMI Skymaster seen here, and a second with the Westinghouse APG-66 in G-MSSA. (Blue Envoy Collection)

Britten-Norman AEW Defender G-MSSA, fitted with the AN/APG-66 radar as used on the General Dynamics F-16, was sent to the US and registered as N360WT for trials. Of note on this aircraft the electro-optical turret fitted under the fuselage. (Blue Envoy Collection)

outsiders, both using the Skymaster AEW radar (a development of the Searchwater from Sea King) were Britten-Norman with the Defender AEW and Airship Industries with the Skyship 600 AEW. The Skymaster radar of the Defender and Skyship lacked power and capability in the role.

Suffice to say, Sentry was ordered and Nimrod AEW3 cancelled. The airframes were sent to Abingdon for reduction to produce, which is MOD parlance for scrapping. The cockpit section of one example, XV259, was for many years displayed at the Solway Aviation Museum at Carlisle Airport but is now in private hands.

The basic problem with the Nimrod AEW3, aside from the change from the original choice of radar type (the FMICW radar had been scrapped in favour of a new pulse-Doppler system), was that it wasn't a Sentry. The Sentry was what the RAF wanted since the Air Staff had first heard of it in the 1960s. Despite it not meeting ASR400 in full, specifically the surface picture aspects, the Boeing E-3 Sentry was ordered in its stead, bringing to an end a process that had lasted from the early 1960s.

To address the shortfall in the surface picture outlined in ASR400, the E-3Ds were later fitted with an enhancement to the AN/APY-1/2 radar's maritime surveillance capability and the RAF's Sentries finally met the requirement for a maritime surface picture in 1995.

The first of six E-3D Sentry AEW1 entered RAF service in 1991, with the option on a seventh being taken up and operated successfully with No 8 Sqn until 2021. Following on from No 8 Sqn's naming of its

All that remains of the Nimrod AEW3 programme is this cockpit section of XV259. Previously on display at the Solway Aviation Museum near Carlisle, it has since been sold to a private owner. (Author)

Just what they always wanted. Always in the background during the Nimrod debacle, the E-3 Sentry was what the Air Staff wanted all along. Six Sentries were ordered in February 1987, with options for another taken up later. No 8 Sqn Sentry AEW1 ZH101 shows off its CFM56 turbofans, Yellow Gate wingtip pods and refuelling probe as it wheels around Mt Rainier on a predelivery photographic sortie. (Blue Envoy Collection)

The changing of the guard. When introduced in 1972, the Shackleton AEW2 was intended to be in service for five years. It was 1991 before the stop-gap Shackleton was relieved of duties by the Sentry AEW1. A No 8 Sqn Sentry, nose up, tries to hold station with Shackleton, WL757, which is going flat out. (Blue Envoy Collection)

The other changing of the guard in the RAF was the transfer of air defence duties from the Phantom FGR2 (XV468 and XT897) to the Tornado F3 (ZE253 and ZG770). The key to improving the air defence of the GIUK Gap was AEW and, from 1991, Sentries such as XH105 provided AEW cover for the interceptors. (Blue Envoy Collection)

Shackleton AEW2s after characters in *The Magic Roundabout*, the seven Sentries were invariably named after Disney's Seven Dwarfs. In addition to the maritime enhancements to the AN/APY-1 radar, the seven Sentry AEW1s were fitted with CFM56 turbofans, Yellow Gate ESM equipment in wingtip pods, thought to be the only components made for Nimrod that found their way onto Sentry. The Sentry also received a refuelling probe above the cockpit, offset to starboard to clear the boom refuelling receptacle, allowing them to refuel from RAF and USAF tankers.

Following the RAF's selection of Sentry, the Armee de l'Air also opted for it, joining forces with the RAF on the development of their respective E-3s. Like the RAF, Armee de l'Air took delivery of its first Sentry in 1991, with the four machines delivered, designated E-3F, also powered by CFM56 turbofans and with capacity to be fitted with a refuelling probe.

It was quite a leap from the growling of the Shackleton AEW2's four Rolls-Royce Griffons and the Chinagraph pencil plots of the AN/APS-20 to the 'shirt-sleeve' environment and lightpens of the Sentry. The workload on the RAF's seven Sentries since March 1991 took its toll and airframes were gradually withdrawn. The last operational sortie by an RAF Sentry was in July 2021 during Operation *Shader*. The Boeing E-7 Wedgetail was due to enter RAF service in 2023, but that appears to be wishful thinking.

Three of the RAF's Sentries have been sold to the Fuerza Aérea de Chile (FACh) to replace its IAI Phalcon. Two examples, ZH103 and ZH106, will be put into service with the FACh while a third, ZH101, will be used as a source of spares. One airframe, ZH104, was flown to the US and inspected by the US Navy before being converted to a training aircraft for the US Navy's E-6 Mercury airborne command post and communications relay aircraft.

Sentry can still be seen in UK airspace, flown by NATO and the USAF, but in 2022, Waddington, home of the RAF's Sentry fleet, hosted a member of the new generation of airborne early warning aircraft – the Gulfstream G550CAEW.

Left: Compared with the contemporary Nimrod AEW3, the Boeing E-3D Sentry AEW1 was spacious and could be walked around without stooping. It was also very much quieter than the Shackleton that No 8 Sqn had been used to. The view looking aft shows the back-to-back consoles for the operators. (Blue Envoy Collection)

Below: The 7° forward tilt of the antenna for the L-band MESA radar allows the Wedgetail to be trimmed in attitude to provide fuel efficiency and thus optimise patrol times. (Australian Department of Defence)

Bottom: The air arm with the longest experience of AEW is the RAF, beginning with the Wellington ACI of 1941 and continuing into the future with the Boeing E-7. (Author)

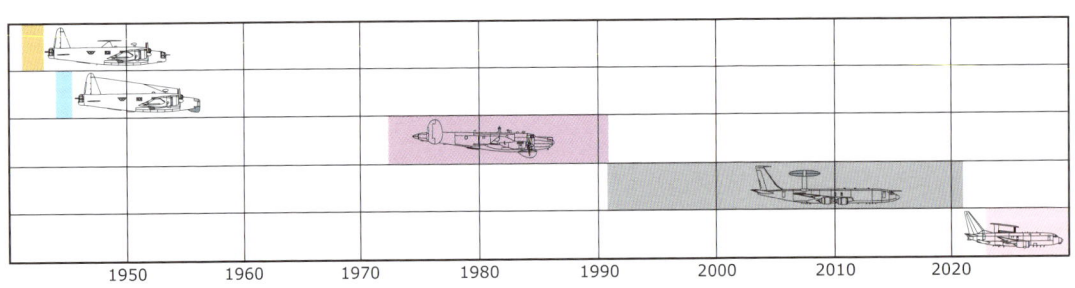

Chapter 8
A New Generation

'The GEC boys demonstrated a situation in which there was clutter. My God, there was clutter. It was impossible to pick up anything. They then switched in the computer — which has only recently been fitted — and the performance improvement was remarkable'. Lewis Carter-Jones MP, parliamentary debate on Nimrod AEW3, 18 December 1986

What destroyed the Nimrod was computing power, or rather the lack of it. The radar system's computers became overloaded by the surface targets that it was required to detect and track, they shut down and restarted. One restriction on computing power was the size of the airframe and the size of the computers, not to mention cooling all the electronics. The Nimrod had been an ideal size when the FMICW radar was in favour, but the higher computer demanded by pulse-Doppler was another matter.

By 1990, a revolution in computer processing power and radar technology brought a new generation of highly effective AEW platforms to market. These were marketed as more than early warning systems, but like the E-3 Sentry were capable of controlling operations and thus were dubbed Airborne Early Warning and Control (AEW&C) systems. Two, in particular, made their debut in 1994 and have since formed the basis of a number of AEW&C systems on the market today: Erieye and Phalcon.

The SAAB/Ericsson S100 Argus was developed for the Swedish Air Force to meet a 1985 requirement and comprised a SAAB SF340 commuter airliner fitted with a dorsal antenna described as a 'balance beam', named after the gymnastics apparatus. The S100's radar is the Erieye, an active electronically scanned array (AESA) radar that dispenses with a conventional rotating scanner and uses the fixed antenna to scan 150° each side of the aircraft track. Detection range is quoted as 220 miles (354km), even under severe clutter conditions and, for Sweden being a maritime nation, a sea surveillance capability.

The prototype installation, a dummy antenna for aerodynamic trials took place in 1985 mounted on a TP 88C, the Swedish designation for the Swearingen Metro III commuterliner. TP 88C 88003 was subsequently fitted with the initial PS-890 Erieye (a contraction of 'Ericsson' and 'eye') radar and tested

The first AEW aircraft in service to use the 'balance beam' antenna was the Saab S100 Argus. As with the Wedgetail's MESA antenna, the balance beam antenna is aligned to allow the aircraft to be trimmed in an aerodynamically efficient attitude while keeping the antenna horizontal. Argus 100006 of the Swedish Air Force shows the modifications made to the SF340. (Blue Envoy Collection)

in 1987. The trials proved successful, so an order was placed for six radar installations to be fitted in the SAAB 340 commuterliner. The system entered service with the Swedish Air Force in 1997 and was designated S100 Argus, named after the Greek deity with 100 eyes.

In addition to service with the Swedish Air Force, Argus has been an export success, having also served with the air forces of Pakistan and Thailand. A larger variant, SAAB 2000 Erieye, was based on the SAAB 2000 airliner and bought by Saudi Arabia, UAE and Bangladesh, while Pakistan replaced its Argus with the SAAB 2000 Erieye.

Greece briefly operated two S100s while awaiting delivery of SAAB's next AEW&C platform, the R-99 Erieye, based on the Embraer EMB-145 commuter jet.

Contemporaneous with the development of Erieye, Israel Aerospace Industries (IAI) and Elta developed the EL/M-2075 Phalcon, an AEW&C system that could be fitted to a variety of aircraft. The system provides 360° coverage and comprises six antennas: two in a fore-and-aft scanner configuration in the nose and tail, plus two large, phased array antennas on each side of the forward fuselage. This has become known as conformal AEW (CAEW) and dispenses with the rotodomes of earlier AEW types.

The initial iteration used the Boeing 707 as its platform and the first customer was the Chilean Air Force, which, on receiving the aircraft in 1993, named it 'Condor'. The Condor lacks the rear antenna, but with

From 1985, Ericsson developed the PS-890 Erieye AEW with the balance beam antenna and in 1987 mounted it for trials on a Fairchild Metro III commuterliner. The trials were successful and led to the Erieye system that was carried by the SAAB SF340 as the S100 Argus. (Blue Envoy Collection)

This Swedish Air Force Argus was one of two. 100003 seen here, was loaned to the Hellenic Air Force pending delivery of its Erieye fleet. (Anthony Mylonakis via Ioannis Mylonas)

the forward and side arrays, coverage of 240° is thought possible, while the Phalcon system can maximise power to one array to provide increased range. The Israeli Air Force procured a pair of Phalcons to replace its fleet of E-2 Hawkeyes. Another benefit arising from the CAEW configuration is that scan speed can be increased electronically, well beyond the rotation speed of a mechanical rotodome.

The Phalcon system can also be configured with its phased array antennas in a 'rotodome' mounted on a pylon above the rear fuselage, as is the case with the EL/W-2090 system, an updated Phalcon fitted to three Ilyushin Il-76 *Candid*s of the Indian Air Force. The antenna suite comprises what appears to be a rotodome, mounted in the same fashion as the Beriev A50 *Mainstay*, but the fixed rotodome houses three phased array antennas arranged around the dish at 120° angles to each other to provide 360° coverage.

Having installed the Phalcon system in the Boeing 707, IAI and Elta took advantage of the advances in computer and radar technology to reduce the size of the system and fit it in a smaller airframe. This resulted in the EL/W-2085 that could be installed in a transcontinental bizjet or small jetliner, modified with fore and aft radomes and large conformal arrays on the forward fuselage.

The shape of things to come. Israeli Aerospace Industries' Phalcon system combined fore and aft mechanically scanned antenna in nose and tail with conformal phased arrays on each side of the forward fuselage. Aside from Israel, only the Chilean Air Force procured Phalcon, which it called Condor. This configuration would be applied to the bizjet generation. (Wiki Commons)

Beriev A-50EI KW-3552 shows the three dielectric sections of the 'fixed rotodome' antenna. Each section covers an AESA antenna for the Israeli EL/W-2090 radar. India acquired two A-50EI while developing the Netra. (Yefim Gordon Archive)

Chapter 9
Bizjet Revolution

'Tell Edward, wheels up in twenty'. Red Reddington, The Blacklist

You know you have 'arrived' when you travel on a 'G'. Calling ahead (or having someone call ahead) to have your G readied for departure in 20 minutes is a decadence few of us will experience. The Gulfstream G series bizjets, and others in its class such as the Bombardier Global, Cessna Citation, Embraer Legacy and Dassault Falcon series epitomised success for decades. They have also been used by air forces to transport top brass and other VIPs since the Lockheed JetStar appeared on the scene in 1961.

In the early 2000s, two arcs of development converged. Bizjets were becoming bigger and marketed as possessing longer range and larger cabins, which could translate into endurance and room to move around. Some were large enough to become commuter airliners plying their trade between the cities of many countries. The other arc was active electronically scanned array (AESA) technology radars and associated systems, the development of which saw AEW radars shrink in size. The convergence meant that the long endurance, roomy bizjets could be fitted with AEW radar as capable as the Sentry and Hawkeye of half a century before.

The helmet illustration shows the groundcrew's pride in an immaculately turned out aircraft. After operating a pair of SAAB S100 Argus, the Hellenic Air Force received four Erieye EMB-145H AEW&C. These are operated by the 380th Airborne Early Warning & Control System Squadron at Elefsina Air Base near Athens. (Anthony Mylonakis via Ioannis Mylonas)

Three companies led this development: Israel Aerospace Industries (IAI) and Elta Electronics Industries in Israel and Saab Electronic Defence Systems (formerly Ericsson Microwave Systems) in Sweden. The Israeli and Swedish companies took different approaches to the process but built on techniques they had honed during the 1980s.

The Israeli approach was to continue with the systems developed for the Boeing 707 Phalcon that served with Israeli and Chilean air forces. Such is the reduction in the size of the EL/W-2075 that rather than a Boeing 707, the EL/W-2085 is compact enough to fit on a Gulfstream G550 bizjet designated the G550CAEW (Conformal Airborne Early Warning). Rather than the six AESA arrays of the EL/M-2075 of the Phalcon, the G550CAEW uses four arrays, one each side of the forward fuselage operating in L-band, one each in nose and tail radomes operating in S-band.

Interestingly, this configuration was considered for the Nimrod AEW with Westinghouse proposing a four-antenna system for Nimrod that combined two 6ft (1.8m) diameter antennas as a FASS with a 24 x 6ft (7.3 x 1.8m) planar array on each side of the forward fuselage. Could the Nimrod have been far more advanced than everyone thinks? This configuration fitted to a compact airframe (Nimrod was compact when compared with the Boeing 707), but unfortunately the computing capacity wasn't sophisticated enough at the time.

The Israeli Air Force acquired a pair of G550CAEW (called Eitam) to replace its Phalcons while Italy's Aeronautica Militare opted for the type as part of an offset deal with Israel on the Aermacchi M-346 trainer for the Israeli Air Force. The Italian G550CAEWs have been in service since 2018 and have taken part in exercises in the UK, offering the RAF its first experience of the new generation of AEW&C in European skies. The type has also been active in monitoring Russian and Ukrainian air operations in Ukraine, Belarus and Russia. Italy has since ordered a further two examples, which brings its fleet to four.

One of the earliest adopters of the bizjet AEW platform was Singapore. The Republic of Singapore Air Force bought four G550AEW (plus one G550 for training) to replace its E-2 Hawkeyes. This example, 018, is operated by No 111 Sqn RSAF. (Author)

This photograph of a RSAF G550CAEW shows the configuration to advantage. The large panels for the side-looking EL/W-2085 radar dominate the airframe. (Wiki Commons)

A No 111 Sqn RSAF G550AEW conducts a twilight flypast in Singapore, with an escort of locally upgraded Northrop F-5S. Singapore operates one of the most modern, and formidable, air forces in the region. The F-5S fleet has been replaced, with the Lockheed Martin F-35 on order. (Wiki Commons)

Singapore, at the hub of many geopolitical disputes, has always believed in strong defences and like its flag carrier airline, operates one of the most modern fleets in the world. A quartet of G550CAEWs ordered in 2008 and declared operational in 2010, replaced the four E-2 Hawkeyes that had been in service since 1987. Interestingly, as well as maintaining an AEW presence in the airspace around Singapore, the Republic of Singapore also operated a Tethered Aerostat Radar System (TARS) equipped with what is thought to be an Israeli radar such as the EL-2022.

Brazilian Balance Beam

The E-99 is the Brazilian Air Force designation for the Erieye radar installed in Embraer's 45-seat regional airliner and provides much improved speed (for deployment) and altitude (for radar coverage) over the original SAAB S100. The E-99 entered service with Brazil in 2001 with the original R-99 redesignated as the E-99 in 2008. It has also been designated as the EMB-145AEW&C and has since been sold to Greece, which operated it during the Libyan Civil War, and to Mexico.

SAAB's next AEW&C system was the GlobalEye, that combines the SAAB Erieye radar and Leonardo Seaspray surface surveillance radar with the Bombardier 6000/6500 bizjet. The Seaspray radar can operate in maritime or terrestrial mode with a synthetic aperture and moving target indicator to provide a standoff battlefield surveillance capability. The GlobalEye can also be operated with only a flight crew aboard, the radars' data transmitted to a ground station via satellite datalink, full circle from Cadillac.

With a typically Greek landscape in the background, a Hellenic Air Force Erieye EMB-145H AEW&C shows how the antenna dominates the aircraft, with the downward angle obvious. Also of note, is the sheer number of antennae on the aircraft. (Anthony Mylonakis via Ioannis Mylonas)

This interesting view of the tail of Hellenic Air Force EMB-145AEW&C 729 shows the number of modifications made to the standard EMB-145. These include strakes carrying radar-warning receivers and finlets on the tailplanes. (Anthony Mylonakis via Ioannis Mylonas)

Aquila audax

In the late 1980s, the Australian government became concerned by the military build-up in countries around South East Asia. The RAAF identified AEW&C as a key role for the future (Australia had not fielded an AEW type) and in 1994 commenced studies that led to Project AIR 5077. This defined the requirement and in 1996 the Australian Department of Defence issued a request for proposals to industry for an AEW&C type to enter service early in the 21st century. This became known as Project Wedgetail, named after the largest bird of prey in Australia, the wedge-tailed eagle, *Aquila audax*.

Boeing was awarded a contract, in 1999, covering four aircraft with an option for a further three. Since any available 707s were too old, rather than offer the AWACS equipment on a Boeing 767 like the E-767 just entering service with the Japanese Air Self Defence Force, Boeing proposed something different that used modern technology in a compact, cheaper package. The proposal was the 737 AEW&C, which was based on the 737-700 airliner and fitted with the Northrop Grumman Electronic Systems Multi-role Electronically Scanned Array (MESA) radar.

The antenna for this has the appearance of a deep rectangular dorsal 'fin', topped with a flat fairing, giving rise to the name 'top hat' for the antenna, but perhaps 'mesa' is the more apt as it looks like the geological feature of the same name. The fairing is angled upwards from its forward to aft end, a configuration designed to minimise drag when the aircraft is at optimum angle of attack while on patrol.

The 35ft 5in x 11ft 2in (10.8 x 3.4m) high antenna assembly incorporates 23ft 11in x 8ft 9in (7.3 x 2.7m) high side-emitting electronic manifold array in the fin, which gives 120° coverage to each side. To complete 360° coverage, the long fairing on top provides fore and aft coverage, 60° from antenna at each end.

The MESA radar can conduct air and sea surveillance, while the system is capable of fighter control and battlespace management operations. A secondary role is ELINT, using the MESA antenna in passive mode.

The type was designated E-7A and the name Wedgetail stuck, becoming the official RAAF name. The first example was delivered in 2010, delayed by radar/computer integration problems (apparently not a feature unique to British AEW projects) with the last of six Wedgetails handed over to No 2 Sqn RAAF in

Above: A RAAF No 2 Sqn E-7A Wedgetail sits in the equatorial sun in Singapore. This side view shows the various changes to the 737 airframe and the number of radomes for the systems the aircraft carries in addition to the dorsal radar. (Author)

Right: The MESA antenna dominates the E-7A. The radar antenna is the large dielectric panel on the side of what appears to be a large pylon. The radomes on each end of the fairing provides the fore and aft coverage. This example, A30-003, of No 2 Sqn RAAF was on display in Singapore in 2018. (Author)

2012. The Wedgetails were soon in action when in April 2014 they acted as the search and rescue (SAR) co-ordination platform in the search for the Malaysian Airlines MH370 in the southern Indian Ocean. By October that year, the Wedgetails were over Iraq operating as part of the coalition against the Islamic State in Iraq alongside RAF and USAF Sentries.

The second customer for the Boeing 737 AEW&C was Turkey, which acquired the type after it beat off stiff opposition from the IAI G550CAEW to win the contract for four aircraft, with an option for a further two. Under the Peace Eagle programme, Turkish Aerospace Industries was the main subcontractor and undertook conversion and testing of the airframes, while HAVELSAN, a Turkish software and systems support contractor undertook testing and support of the computer systems. As with the RAAF's examples, deliveries were delayed due to various aspects of the systems' integrations and development.

The first 737 AEW&C was delivered to the Türk Hava Kuvvetleri (Turkish Air Force) in February 2015 while the last of the original quartet was delivered in December 2015. The type, like all NATO AEW and surveillance assets, has been involved in monitoring Russian and Ukrainian forces since February 2022. The Türk Hava Kuvvetleri's Peace Eagles have been operating along the Poland/Belarus and Poland/Ukraine borders.

Another customer for the E-7A is South Korea; its air force also looked at the Gulfstream G550CAEW, but ordered four E-7As under the Peace Eye programme. Boeing subcontracted Korean Aerospace Industries to perform the modifications and installation with all four delivered by late 2012.

None of the initial customers for the E-7A had operated AEW aircraft before, but there then arose the question of replacing the AEW aircraft of air forces that had. As noted in Chapter 7, the RAF's Sentries had been worked hard and when the option to upgrade to the USAF's Block 40/45 standard (under Project Eagle) was declined by the MOD in 2009, this effectively placed a limit on the Sentry AEW1's operational life. Despite this, the UK government stated in its 2015 defence review that the type would remain in service until 2035. Reality was very different, and towards the end of 2020, reports in *Air Forces Monthly* stated that only two Sentries were available at any time!

This issue was addressed in October 2018 when the MOD declared an intention to buy the E-7A, with an order for five examples being placed in March 2019. The deal drew significant criticism as there had been no competitive tendering for the contract. SAAB cried foul, as its Erieye system was just as capable and could be mounted on the Airbus A330 MRTT, a version of which was already in service with the RAF.

Despite the hoo-ha, particularly about the size of the fleet, the procurement process continued with STS Aviation Group at Birmingham Airport selected to carry out the modifications and installation for the RAF E-7As, which would be designated Wedgetail AEW1. Always on the lookout for a saving the MOD opted to convert a pair of former airline Boeing 737s while the rest would be new builds.

That was the situation until early 2021 when that year's Integrated Defence Review reduced the procurement to three aircraft! Three Wedgetails would effectively mean that one would be used for training, one would be undergoing maintenance and one would be available for operations. Then, in light of the war in Ukraine, a further defence review reinstated the two cancelled E-7s.

Once in service, the E-7s will be based at Lossiemouth on the Moray Firth, alongside the RAF's Boeing P-8A Poseidon MRA1 fleet, which shares the Boeing 737 lineage. The MOD has stated that the E-7A will be called Wedgetail AEW1 in RAF service. It will invariably become known as the 'Wedgie', which conjures up images of rugby field japes.

A shape that will become as familiar to the population of the area around the Moray Firth as the Shackleton was four decades before, the Boeing E-7A Wedgetail 'fleet' will be based, like the Shackletons, at RAF Lossiemouth. (John Lee/Central Queensland Plane Spotting)

Chapter 10
Patrolling the Arctic – Soviet AEW

'Сами не летаем – другим не дадим' meaning 'Don't fly – don't let others / If we can't fly – we won't let anyone else either' was the unofficial motto of the войска ПВО - voyska protivovozdushnoy oborony (V-PVO) –the Anti-Air Defence Troops of the Soviet Armed Forces.

Until the early 1990s, aside from the UK and US, the only other nation with air forces fielding an AEW aircraft was the Soviet Union, a vast landmass that extended over 11 time zones. The northern areas of the USSR were expanses of taiga and tundra leading to the Arctic Ocean, across which American bombers or missiles could appear at any moment. Similarly, the southern regions of the Soviet Union required coverage to avoid a surprise attack.

Like the Americans, the Soviets built a series of radar stations across the north, to watch for signs of attacks and to track the activities of the USAF's reconnaissance aircraft. A network of stations to cover the northern areas of the Soviet Union would be prohibitively expensive so, like the Americans, the Soviets had numerous gaps in the coverage and sought to fill these with airborne radars. In 1968, a Soviet documentary film showed an amazing aircraft, a Tupolev Tu-114 *Cleat* airliner with a massive rotodome mounted on a dorsal pylon on the rear fuselage. This was the West's first sight of the Tu-126 airborne

Beriev A-100 *Mainstay* prototype 78651 in service colours on approach to landing. The most obvious differences from the earlier *Mainstays* are the larger diameter PS-90A turbofans, electronic countermeasure (ECM) pods under the wingtips and an ECM fairing above the cockpit. (Yefim Gordon Archive)

early warning aircraft that was soon assigned the ASCC reporting name *Moss*. The Tu-126 was the result of a late 1950s attempt to fit an AEW&C system in a Tu-95 *Bear*, which not only lacked the space for the equipment, but being crammed in, the equipment overheated. Nor did the *Bear* have the room to accommodate the requisite number of operators, so like the Americans with the Sentry, the Soviets opted to use an airliner and the largest available at the time (and in the world) was the Tupolev Tu-114 *Cleat*. The *Cleat* had the space and the endurance for the role and when fitted with an air-to-air refuelling probe could cover the expanses of northern Siberia and the Arctic.

The radar, with its antenna mounted in a large dorsal rotodome, was called Liana (known to NATO as *Flapjack*) and Western pundits took great delight in pointing out that it only worked over the sea, either omitting or unaware that NATO radars of similar vintage only worked over the sea. The eight-bladed contraprops that propelled the *Moss* also affected radar performance, but this was apparently fixed by replacing the metal blades with glass reinforced plastic, which was also done by the West on its AEW aircraft. As noted above, the British FMICW radar could not be used with propellers unless the metal blades were substituted for plastic. In the case of *Moss*, the solution was a new radar called Shmel that would be used on the Tu-126's replacement – the Beriev A-50.

The Tu-126 made its first flight in 1962 and entered service in 1965, but apparently Western analysts only became aware of it in 1968, in the aforementioned documentary. Twelve Tu-126 *Moss* were built, and the type remained in service until replaced by the Beriev A-50 *Mainstay* in 1984.

Having examined the Tu-116D passenger variant of Tu-95 *Bear* with a view to using it for AEW, the roomier Tu-114 *Cleat* was selected for conversion to AEW. The *Cleat* was the largest and fastest airliner when introduced and has held the record for fastest propeller-driven aircraft since 1960. It was a spectacular beast, as were the boarding steps. (Blue Envoy Collection)

A US Navy F-4B Phantom holds station with a Tu-126 *Moss*. When it first appeared in a Soviet propaganda film it took the West by surprise. Throughout the 1970s, it was derided in the West as only able to operate over water. Of note here is the dark area on the forward fuselage, which is reinforcement to protect the fuselage skinning from ice shed from the propellers. (Blue Envoy Collection)

The *Moss* was a fairly regular 'customer' for the Swedish Air Force quick reaction alert squadrons. Very few Tu-126s carried bort numbers and this unmarked Tu-126 was intercepted by a Swedish Air Force J35 Drakens over the Baltic. (Yefim Gordon Archive)

The Beriev A-50 could be described as the logical outcome of a search for a Tu-126 *Moss* replacement – jet-powered, capacious fuselage and the endurance to match the mission requirement. The A-50, known to NATO as *Mainstay* could be described as comparable with the Boeing E-3 Sentry when it entered service in 1984. The A-50 is based on the Ilyushin Il-76 *Candid* transport modified to incorporate cooling systems and heat exchangers in the undercarriage sponsons and a large dorsal rotodome for the Shmel radar mounted on the rear fuselage.

The A-50 is in service with the Russian Air Force and has seen action in the Syrian Civil War and Russia's invasion of and subsequent war on Ukraine, while the Indian Air Force operates the A-50EI fitted with the Israeli EL/W-2090 system. A number of Il-76 *Candid* airframes have been modified with rotodomes and while they may look like A-50 *Mainstay*s these are in fact specialist monitoring aircraft. Known as СКИП – Самолетный Контрольно-Измерительный Пункт, (SKIP – Airborne Check Measure and Control Centre) these are used to monitor trials of new equipment, such as cruise missiles.

As with any AEW&C type, the *Mainstay* has been upgraded, with a major refurbishment including replacement of analogue systems with digital and in recent years, the Shmel radar has been replaced with the Shmel-2 radar, with the result being designated the A-50M. The ultimate A-50 was the A-50U, fitted with the Shmel-M radar systems and new displays.

The A-50U led to the Beriev A-100 with 'double the capability' according to Beriev. Based on the Il-76MD-90A, which is a modernised Il-76 *Candid*, the A-100 comes equipped with a 'glass' cockpit, upgraded avionics, a composite wing structure and Aviadvigatel PS-90A-76 turbofans. The Shmel-M radar has been replaced with the Premier system, which uses an electronically scanned (in elevation) phased-array antenna. The rotodome still rotates, to scan in azimuth but at 12rpm, double that of the Sentry. The Beriev A-100 is also credited with a ground surveillance capability, but this has yet to be confirmed. (See Appendix 3)

An impressive sight as it unsticks in a cloud of snow at the Zhukovsky test centre, this Tu-126LL *Moss* was used as an avionics testbed for the *Mainstay*'s Shmel radar system. The main difference from an operational *Moss* is the pod for a heat exchanger under the rear fuselage. (Yefim Gordon Archive)

NATO was aware that a new Soviet AEW aircraft was in development and intelligence provided by an agent suggested it was based on the Ilyushin Il-76 Candid transport. What turned out to be the Beriev A-50 Mainstay was encountered by Royal Norwegian Air Force in the mid-1980s. (Yefim Gordon Archive)

AEW aircraft are generally teamed with interceptors, in this case a Beriev A-50 Mainstay with four Sukhoi Su-27 Flankers. For the long-range air defence of the Rodina's northern regions, the Mainstay would work with the MiG-31 Foxhound. (Blue Envoy Collection)

Above: Beriev A-50U 'Red 41' Taganrog was operated over Syria during Russian operations in that country. This view on the *Mainstay* shows how the original nose glazing of the *Candid* has been replaced with dielectric panels. (Yefim Gordon Archive)

Left: The Beriev A-50M and A-50U were fitted with modern flat-screen displays and computer systems. These replaced the cathode ray tube displays of the original aircraft. (Yefim Gordon Archive)

Interestingly, the Soviets took a different view of AEW operations to that of the NATO nations. Soviet air forces were split into air defence: PVO – Voyska protivovozdushnoy oborony or Voyska PVO; Long range Aviation: VVS-DA – Voenno-Vozdushnye Sily Dal'naya Aviatsiya and Frontal Aviation: VVS-FA – Voenno-Vozdushnye Sily Frontovaya Aviatsiya. Voyska PVO operated the A-50 fleet to defend the Motherland, while Frontal Aviation required a more flexible, if not agile (compared with the A-50), platform to co-ordinate fighters and attack aircraft over the battlefield.

The Antonov Design Bureau at Kyiv modified its An-72 *Coaler* tactical transport to produce a novel design, the An-71 *Madcap*. The rear fuselage was extensively modified to remove the loading ramp and

Not a *Mainstay*, but one of the many Il-76 *Candid*s fitted with rotodomes and electronics pods for monitoring missile and aircraft tests. CCCP-75456 is an IL-76 SKIP (Airborne Check-Measure-and-Control Center) *Candid*, one of five built and operated by the Gromov Flight Institute on behalf of the Russian Ministry of Defence. (Blue Envoy Collection)

The latest iteration of the Beriev *Mainstay* is the A-100. Said to have double the capability of the earlier A-50s, the A-100 is fitted with the Premier radar that combines mechanical scanning in azimuth, with the rotodome rotating at 12rpm, while scanning in elevation is electronic. This prototype is still in primer on its maiden flight. (Yefim Gordon Archive)

When the Antonov An-71 was first seen (in the background of a photo of General Secretary Mikhail Gorbachev visiting the factory), it caused confusion. It was thought to be a carrier borne AEW platform and thanks to its configuration was assigned the NATO reporting name *Madcap*. This example, CCCP-780151, is in Aeroflot colours. (Yefim Gordon Archive)

allow installation of a third engine to provide an extra boost on take-off from forward airfields. The most obvious change from the *Coaler* was the empennage. The *Coaler*'s T-tail was removed, and the tailplanes moved to the rear fuselage while the fin was much enlarged, swept forward and now serving as a support pylon for the rotodome for the *Kvant* radar. The reason for the forward sweep on the fin/pylon was to maintain centre of gravity with the heavy rotodome assembly.

The An-71 made its first flight in 1985 but was subsequently cancelled when the Soviet Union was dissolved in 1991. Western speculation that the An-71 was a carrier-based AEW type in similar vein to the Grumman E-2 Hawkeye proved wide of the mark although Antonov did propose a carrier variant called An-75, which may have moved the two engines to underwing pylons to ease handling on deck and when struck below decks. The real maritime AEW design did exist but came from a different design bureau.

Maritime AEW

The Soviet aspiration for a blue water navy complete with aircraft carriers came to fruition with the commissioning of the *Admiral Kuznetsov* in 1991. Along with its sister ship, *Varyag* (since sold on and commissioned by China), these 'aircraft carrying cruisers' were to be equipped with naval variants of the MiG-29 (*Fulcrum-D*) and Su-27 (*Flanker-D*) with ASW, SAR and Utility roles undertaken by variants of the Kamov Ka-32 *Helix*. Well aware that some form of AEW platform was required and impressed by the Grumman E-2C Hawkeye, a carrier-borne AEW&C aircraft was specified.

The type selected was the Yakovlev Yak-44E, which shared its configuration with the Hawkeye; twin turboprop, endplate fins and a dorsal rotodome for its *Kvant KS*. Unlike the Hawkeye, the rotodome was mounted above the rear fuselage, which was more reminiscent of the Vought V404 that was tendered against the Hawkeye or the 1960s British design studies for naval AEW aircraft for NASR6166. One area where the Yak-44E differed from the Hawkeye was the engines, Progress D27s, with more than twice the power of the Hawkeye's Allison T56. The D27s drove contraprops (described as propfans in some sources) that, in order to reduce acoustic effects, had eight blades on the front propeller and six on the rear. The reason for the greatly increased power was the use of ski-jumps (or even unassisted deck launches) on Soviet carriers rather than catapults. The Yak-44E reached full-scale mock-up stage before being cancelled, with the mock-up being used for handling trials aboard the *Admiral Kuznetzov*.

What did go to sea with the Soviet and Russian fleet took the same approach as the British, an AEW&C platform based on a helicopter. For the Russians, that helicopter was a variant of the Kamov Ka-29 *Helix*-B, an assault transport that shared its dynamics with the Kamov Ka-27 *Helix*-A anti-submarine helicopter. The more capacious cabin of the *Helix*-B made it a better prospect for conversion to an AEW platform and this became the Ka-31 also known as the Ka-252RLD (radiolokatsyonnogo dozora – radar picket).

The large planar array antenna for the E-801M *Oko* (Eye) radar is ventrally mounted and has been designed to fold up to the starboard side and lie flat against the helicopter's underside. To ensure clearance

While the An-71 was being touted in the West as the Soviet equivalent of the Hawkeye, the actual aircraft was the Yak-44. A full-scale mock-up was built, and it incorporated some novel features for the late 1980s. The rotodome could be lowered almost all the way to the top of the fuselage, but of most interest was the propulsion system – two 14,000shp (10,290kW) Muravchenko D-27 turboprops with contra-rotating propellers with eight blades on the front and six blades on the back. (Yefim Gordon Archive)

The mock-up was lifted onto the deck of the *Admiral Kuznetsov* for handling trials. The wings are folded across the fuselage and, concealed beneath a camouflage net, is the rotodome in the fully lowered position. The Yak-44 was almost identical in size to the E-2 Hawkeye. Despite this, the Yak-44's engines were rated at almost three times the power of the E-2, to provide power for ski-jump launch. (Yefim Gordon Archive)

The Russian, Chinese and Indian navies use a rotary wing AEW platform in the form of the Kamov Ka-31 *Helix*. The antenna, seen here deployed, folds upwards through 90° to lie flush under the cabin. (Wiki Commons)

for the rotating antenna, the Ka-31's undercarriage can be raised (retract does not seem apt in this case) to clear the rotation arc of the antenna. One aspect of the Ka-31's configuration that intrigues this author is drag cycling. When Westland Helicopters investigated an AEW variant of the Sea King in the 1970s, one reason it dismissed a large ventral antenna was the effect on the helicopter's handling caused by the cyclic changes in drag as the antenna turned.

The Ka-31 became operational with the navies of Russia in 1995 and India from 2003. At time of writing, the People's Liberation Army Air Force (PLAAF) was introducing the Ka-31, having ordered it in 2013.

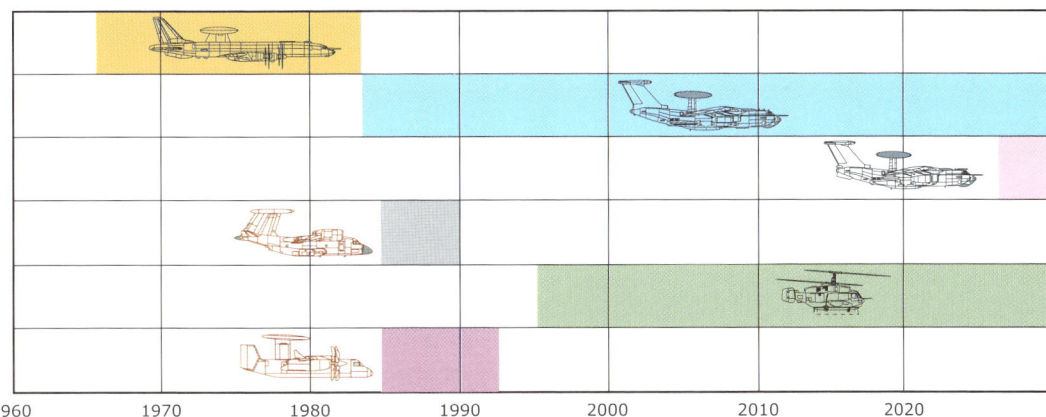

The Soviet Union opted for AEW aircraft to patrol the expanses of the taiga and Arctic Ocean. The Tu-126 *Moss* is possibly one of the most spectacular aircraft to serve in any air arm while the A-50 *Mainstay* has been extensively upgraded, culminating in the A-100. (Author)

Chapter 11
China and India

'Everything. Everywhere. All at Once'. – The PLAAF's approach to AEW

In the field of AEW, one country has tried everything – China. The People's Republic has at some time examined and, aside from the conformal antenna, even built, prototypes of every variation in AEW configuration, be it fore-and-aft scanner, rotodome, AESA in rotodome or balance beam. Rather than opting for a single configuration, the PLAAF and People's Liberation Army Navy (PLAN) has fielded them all. All at once.

China, like the Soviet Union, is vast (despite 'covering' five zones, it operates under a single time zone) and faced a similar problem of radar coverage. Therefore in 1969, the People's Liberation Army Air Force embarked on Project 926, which involved fitting an AEW radar, with a rotodome in a Tupolev Tu-4 *Bull* bomber (an unlicensed, Soviet-built copy of the Boeing B-29). Designated Kong Jing 1, the aircraft conducted a series of trials starting in 1971. Sources stated that the radar system was too heavy and even after replacing the original Shvetsov ASh-73TK piston engines with Ivchenko AI-20K turboprops from an Antonov An-12 *Cub*, still proved incapable of operating. Interestingly, some sources state that two KJ-1s were produced and their role was to monitor US activity in the Pacific.

In the late 1980s and early 1990s, as China opened up economically, the PLAAF looked at AEW again, even at one point showing great interest in the Marconi Argus system, which was the marketing name for an AEW installation based on the MSA used on the Nimrod AEW3. The Shaanxi Y-8J is yet another example of China's many and varied AEW systems based on the Shaanxi Y-8 transport. It comprises a British GEC-Marconi Argus 2000 radar (or a Racal Skymaster) with the antenna housed in a large nose radome.

One radar engineer told this author that: 'The Chinese were great window-shoppers. They showed great interest in everything, but rarely coughed up the cash.' What followed, from the mid-1990s, can only be described as an AEW aircraft equivalent of the Cambrian explosion.

In service, the Netra operates alongside the Indian Air Force's Sukhoi Su-30MKI. The Netra saw action in the Balakot airstrike in February 2019, directing the strikes against suspected terrorist training camps. (Indian Government)

Not a *Mainstay* either, but a *Mainring*, the Xi'An KJ-2000 AEW&C platform is one of the many AEW types operated by the PLAAF. The aircraft is fitted with a fixed rotodome featuring three AESA antennas each scanning a 120° sector around the aircraft. This *Mainring* 30072, is on the strength of the 26th Division of the PLAAF. (Blue Envoy Collection)

The PLAAF eventually reached a conclusion on its AEW capability and opted, in 1997, for the Beriev A-50EI from Russia…but…with an Israeli Elta Phalcon AESA radar, comprising three phased array antennas arranged in an equilateral triangle configuration in the rotodome. Unfortunately, the US government took a dim view of China acquiring such a hi-tech system and forced Israel to withdraw from the agreement. Despite removal of all the kit, the A-50 was flown back to China. Following the break with Israel, the Nanjing Institute of Electronic Technology developed a radar system rather similar to the Phalcon and installed that on four A-50 airframes to produce the Kong Jing 2000. Assigned the ASCC reporting name *Mainring,* the KJ-2000 entered service with the PLAAF in 2007.

Meanwhile, the agreement with Russia to supply Ilyushin Il-76 *Candid* airframes for conversion to KJ-2000 AEW platforms had fallen through, so an indigenous airframe was examined. The Xi'an Y-8, a Chinese-built design based on the Antonov An-12 *Cub*, was fitted with a Erieye-style balance beam antenna. Other modifications included reworking of the rear fuselage to remove the loading ramp, finlets on the ends of the tailplanes and a new unglazed nose. These became known as Kong Jing 200 (KJ-200) or Y-8WH to the PLAAF.

The Xi'an Y-8 also formed the basis of a further AEW variant, which may predate the KJ-2000, this time fitted with a pylon-mounted rotodome just aft of the wing box. This was short-lived as once the AESA radar had been developed for the KJ-2000, the same three-antenna system was fitted in the 'rotodome' to produce the Kong Jing 500 (KJ-500).

China has tried every type of AEW antenna and radar system. This Xian KJ-200 AEW 30176 of 76th ACACR PLAAF is fitted with the balance beam antenna. The type has been assigned the ASCC reporting name *Moth*. (Blue Envoy Collection)

Another of the PLAAF's AEW types is the Shaanxi KJ-200, with the NATO reporting name *Moth*, and features a balance beam antenna atop a Shaanxi Y-8 transport. This *Moth* 30176 is operated by the 76th ACACR, PLAAF. (Blue Envoy Collection)

Naval AEW

Having shown an interest in the Marconi Argus system, the People's Liberation Army Navy (PLAN) actually acquired a similar system, the Racal Skymaster, a derivative of the Searchwater radar used on the Nimrod MR2 and Sea King AEW2. The Skymaster was installed in a large nose radome on a Xi'an Y-8J and thanks to the Y-8's nose up stance on the ground, the radome could be large enough to provide 360° coverage from the single antenna. Eight examples (China had bought eight Skymaster radars) were built, with the first entering service sometime after the Y-8J's first flight in 1998.

The PLAN's blue water navy ambitions match those of the Soviet Union in the 1980s and the PLAN has sought a carrier capability. This has included buying the former Soviet Navy's *Kuznetzov*-class carrier *Varyag* from the Ukraine. The *Varyag* had lain unfinished and was towed to China where it was completed and commissioned as the *Liaoning*.

Since AEW coverage is a must-have capability of a modern navy, the PLAN took a two-pronged approach. Before commissioning a carrier, the PLAN developed a helicopter-borne AEW system based on the Changhe Z-8, a Chinese-built Aerospatiale Super Frelon, which carried an AESA radar with a planar array antenna in the rear cabin. The antenna is deployed out of the Z-8's rear ramp and the machine has been designated Z-18J and called 'Black Bat'. The other helicopter used for AEW by the PLAN is the Kamov Ka-31 *Helix*-B, purchased from Russia, but is considered as a stopgap until the Z-18J Black Bat is fully developed.

The last AEW type associated with the PLAN is a fixed-wing AEW type for use on the service's carriers. Still under development at the time of writing, the Kong Jing 600 (KJ-600) a much-modified Xi'an Y-7 (Chinese-built Antonov An-24). The prototype for the KJ-600 is the JZY-01, which has been modified to carry a dorsal rotodome and a new quadruple fin empennage in what is yet again a Hawkeye analogue.

Despite the secrecy associated with the development of AEW radars and China's military in general, its development work on AEW outstrips any other nation. It could be said that the work has lacked direction but the PLAN and PLAAF has examined every aspect of the role and no doubt at some time a conformal AEW platform will appear.

India

While the UK was struggling with the Nimrod AEW3, India was conducting research for an AEW aircraft. The initial result was a testbed developed by Hindustan Aeronautics based on an HS748 transport with a large dorsal rotodome. The HS748AEW took to the skies in 1988 but by 1990 the Indian

While technically not a *Mainstay* this Indian Air Force Il-76 *Candid* is fitted with the IAI/Elta EL/W-2090 Phalcon system in a non-rotating rotodome. The three sections with the three antenna are just visible in this view of the rotodome. (Michael Sender/Wiki Commons)

India has had an active AEW development programme since the 1980s, culminating in the Defence Research and Development Organisation (DRDO) Netra, which comprises a balance beam AESA radar developed by the Electronics and Radar Development Establishment at Bengaluru mounted on a much-modified Embraer EMB-145 airliner. (Indian government)

government opted to acquire a platform based on the Ilyushin Il-76, but with PS-90 engines and Israeli EL/W-2090 Phalcon AESA radar with three antennas in the fixed rotodome. Two *Candid* Phalcons were acquired but the main effort on AEW in India was indigenous.

The Defence Research and Development Organisation (DRDO) was tasked with developing an AEW&C for the Indian Air Force to complement the *Mainstay*. Rather than rely on foreign sources for the radar, the Electronics and Radar Development Establishment (LRDE) developed a back-to-back planar array AESA antenna with the same balance bar configuration as the SAAB Erieye. The radar, antenna and associated systems were installed on an Embraer EMB-145i, complete with suitable aerodynamic modifications, with the initial integration carried out by Embraer in Brazil.

Known as the Netra AEW&CS, (Netra is the Hindi word for 'Eye') the platform was delivered to the Indian Air Force in 2012 and saw operational service during the Balakot airstrike against suspected terrorist bases in Pakistan in February 2019. Development of the Netra has continued, but the Indian Air Force has discussed fitting the DRDO AEW&CS to other aircraft, namely the EADS C-295 transport and the Airbus A330, which would double as a tanker and AEW platform.

Pakistan

The Pakistan Air Force (PAF) has operated the SAAB Erieye system mounted on the SAAB 2000 commuterliner, which has increased endurance compared with the smaller SF-340-based S100 Argus. The PAF also operates the Chinese ZDK-03, a variant of the Y-8F-600 fitted with an AESA radar developed specifically for it.

Chapter 12

Useful Clutter – Battlefield Surveillance and Radar Reconnaissance

Green Porridge – Aircrew nickname for the H2S display on the V-bombers.

As noted in Chapter 1, AEW had its origins in radars designed to find targets – ships and cities – on the sea or on the landscape. ACI started out as a means to find ships, while ASV Mk VI used in Operations *Cork* and *Elgar*, such as the AN/APS-20 used in Cadillac and beyond were designed for anti-submarine tasks.

Rather than being the clutter that dogged AEW radars, specially designed ground-mapping radars (British sets could trace their lineage back to the H2S radars of 1943) relied on the clutter for target location and navigation. Ground-mapping radar continued to prove useful for targeting and reconnaissance purposes, ultimately with H2S Mk 9 on the *Black Buck* Vulcans in 1982. Air forces around the world invested in radar reconnaissance systems to provide reference data for nuclear strikes. Before ballistic missiles became deterrence's weapon of choice, freefall weapons and aircraft to deliver them were the means of deterrent. To use modern parlance, deterrence is a 24/7 business and in the 1950s the only way to aim bombs in the dark or in cloudy conditions was radar.

Victor B1 XA918 takes off carrying Red Neck in the 40ft-(12m-) long underwing pods. Bending and flexing of the antennae in the pods reduced resolution and therefore its utility so Red Neck was cancelled. (Terry Panopalis Collection)

Bomber navigators would be provided with reference photographs of their target and prominent features on the approach route, as it would be displayed on the radar display as the bomber approached target. This targeting system relied on having a reference photograph in the first place and how the approach would appear on the navigator's display. To achieve that, air forces developed radar reconnaissance aircraft that could fly over the targets before the strike mission (either just prior to or a long time before) and capture images of the radar display on camera. This navigation and weapons-aiming method and subsequent use of similar systems in reconnaissance were much favoured by the British.

One of the foremost projects in the radar reconnaissance role was the RAF's R156, a Mach 3 aircraft to carry a Red Drover radar. It was a cutting-edge requirement that pushed British aircraft design, construction and instrumentation (this was before such things were called avionics) to the limit. The engine developers were also taxed as the turbojets had to be capable of cruising at Mach 2.5 with 'bursts' up to Mach 3.

Operational Requirement OR330, issued to the aircraft companies in 1954, called for a high speed/high altitude aircraft that could operate beyond the reach of Soviet air defences, which at that point comprised interceptor aircraft and anti-aircraft guns. Much has been written on the subsequent bomber version, RB156, that was under development as the Avro 730, but the radar reconnaissance aspects have rarely been addressed. Many designs were submitted for R156, with the two front-runners being Avro's

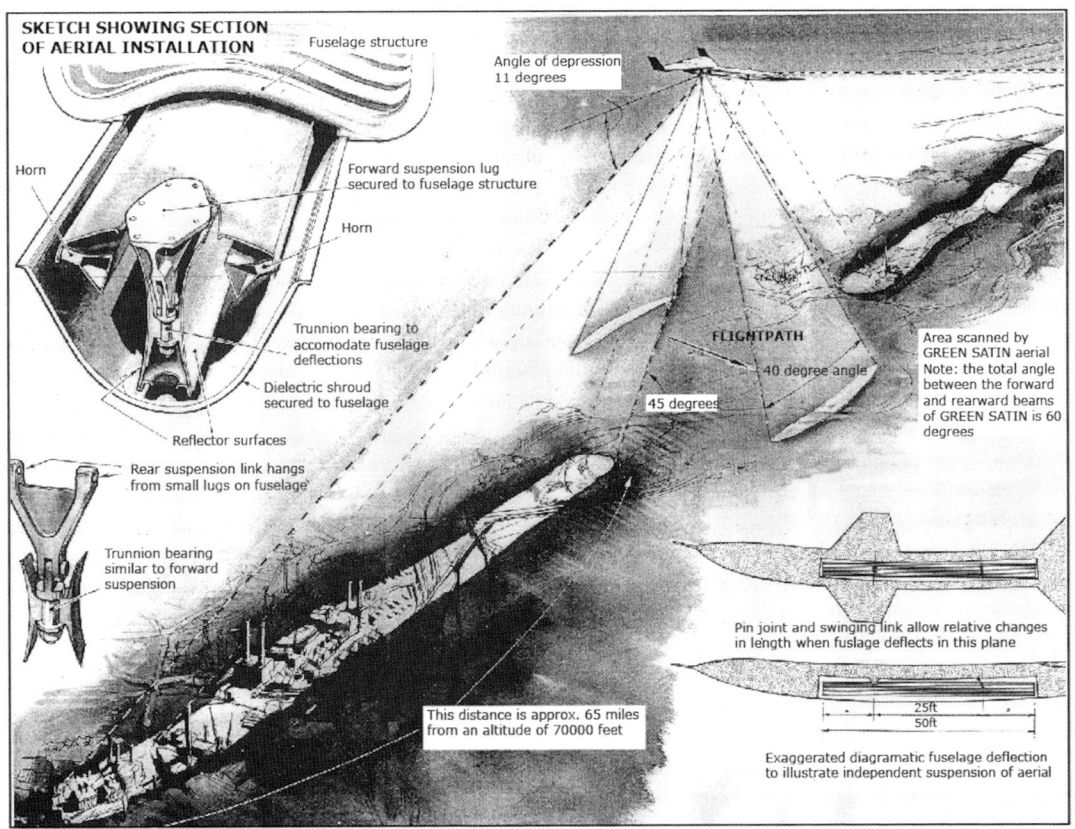

The Mach 3 radar reconnaissance aircraft to meet R.156 was to survey a swathe of ground up to 65 miles (105km) each side of the flight path. This diagram shows the EMI version of Red Drover under development for the Vickers SP4 aircraft. (Brooklands Museum)

Type 730 (the eventual winner of the bomber competition) and the Vickers SP4. Both were designed around the antennae of a radar called Red Drover.

The intention of Red Drover and the R156 aircraft was to prepare radar maps of routes into the Soviet Union and allow the V-Force to follow these predetermined tracks, by day or night, with great accuracy on their own radars. The primary sensor, the Red Drover ground-mapping radar, initially operated in the X-band but this was later changed to J-band. It used a pair of 50ft (15.2m) long antennae arranged along the lower fuselage sides, which in turn drove the configuration of the aircraft. Such a radar would become known as a sideways-looking airborne radar (SLAR).

As a navigation aid, it was essentially a very refined form of dead reckoning as the V-bombers used H2S Mk 9 radars that would provide a different radar image to the SLAR. Fortunately, ground features such as lakes, rivers and urban areas produced radar returns that could be readily identified from their shapes. This allowed the navigator to compare the 'green porridge' on the bomber's radar display with the photographs of the Red Drover display.

These long antennae looked downwards and to the side of the aircraft's ground track, producing a radar 'picture' comprising a strip of returns on each side of the aircraft track. Two versions of Red Drover were under development: one by EMI for the Avro 730 and the other by Vickers' inhouse radar department for their SP4. The Vickers Red Drover antennae used two back-to-back parabolic reflectors 50ft (15.2m) long mounted on a central beam. At each side of the central beam, directed inwards onto each reflector at an angle, was a 50ft (15.2m) long horn transmitter/receiver. This meant that the reflectors could be mounted to allow for movement of the aircraft structure.

For the Avro Type 730, EMI's Red Drover did not use a central reflector but larger transmit/receive horns directed outwards and downwards. The Vickers version may have been a more compact installation but could a 50ft (15.2m) long radar be described as compact?

Also launched in 1954 was the Blue Steel stand-off missile that would carry the British nuclear deterrent, but used inertial navigation and therefore did not need the radar images. Another burgeoning problem was the improvements to Soviet air defences with the development of the S-25 Berkut (SA-1 *Guild*) and S-75 Dvina (SA-2 *Guideline*) plus interceptors such as the MiG-19 *Farmer* and Yakovlev Yak-25 *Flashlight* armed with Kaliningrad K-5 (AA-1 *Alkali*) air-to-air missiles. The threat was such and the hopes high for the Blue Steel that the Air Staff cancelled the supersonic Avro 730 in early 1957. Note that this project was cancelled before the 1957 (Sandys) Defence White Paper was published.

Victor B1 XA918 showing the Red Neck pods. The two pods of Red Neck housed different SLARs. The port wing pod carried an X-band radar with a 30ft (9.1m) antenna while the starboard pod carried a Q-band radar with a 15ft (4.55m) antenna. (Terry Panopalis Collection)

Useful Clutter – Battlefield Surveillance and Radar Reconnaissance

With the cancellation of the supersonic radar reconnaissance aircraft, attention turned to fitting the V-bombers with a similar capability. This work led to the development of a system called Red Neck, a high resolution SLAR to be used by the Handley Page Victors of the Radar Reconnaissance Force (RRF). Housed in a pair of 40ft (12.2m) long pods mounted under the outer wings of a Victor, Red Neck comprised two radars; an X-band with a 30ft (9.1m) antenna in the port wing pod while the starboard pod carried a Q-band radar with a 15ft (4.55m) antenna.

Meanwhile, a pulsed radar system called Green Satin had been developed as a navigation aid for Canberra bombers and the V-force. Green Satin used Doppler techniques and could produce accurate ground speed and provide the amount of drift due to wind, which up to this point had always been difficult to determine. When combined with the bomber's H2S Mk 9A radar, a useful SLAR-type system called Red Setter was produced by using the Green Satin data to keep the H2S antenna normal to the aircraft's ground track rather than rotating. This technique was used for radar reconnaissance sorties by Handley Page Victor K2s during the Falklands War.

Right: With the cancellation of Red Neck, the V-force used its H2S Mk.9A radar and Green Satin doppler system for radar reconnaissance. This is the antenna of the H2S Mk.9A as fitted to Vulcan and Victor. On the Victor, this combination was known as Red Setter and remained in service until 1993. (Author)

Below: RAF Germany used the McDonnell Douglas F-4M Phantom FGR2 for battlefield reconnaissance using the EMI reconnaissance pod. This pod is the large store on the Phantom's centreline, with the antennas for the P.391 Radar visible as dark dielectric panels on the pod. (Terry Panopalis Collection)

The EMI P391 sideways-looking airborne radar fitted to the reconnaissance pod of the Phantom FGR2 produced an image of the terrain to each side of the aircraft's track. The black strip across the image is the blind spot below the aircraft. The P.391 had been developed for TSR2 but was subsequently pod-mounted for the Phantom. (Blue Envoy Collection)

Responsibility for the UK deterrent had, by 1969, been transferred to the Royal Navy and its Polaris missile-armed *Resolution* class submarines. There was no pressing need for a strategic radar reconnaissance capability, but SLARs were being considered for tactical use as a reconnaissance asset rather than as a navigation aid. The famous BAC TSR2 was to carry an EMI P.391 Q-band SLAR, initially as a navigation aid, but as the designation suggests, later as a reconnaissance sensor. The P.391's development continued after TSR2 was cancelled, finally appearing in the EMI reconnaissance pod used by McDonnell Douglas Phantom FGR2s while they were engaged in the ground attack role in West Germany. On the Phantom's replacement in the reconnaissance role by the SEPECAT Jaguar GR1, the P.391 was not fitted in BAC's reconnaissance pod for the Jaguar due to reliability problems.

US Radar Reconnaissance

Like the RAF, the USAF favoured radar reconnaissance in the early days of the Cold War. Strategic Air Command fitted 16 Boeing RB-47s with SLARs for the *Peter Pan* programme that involved overflights of Soviet territory. The results were promising, with targets such as airfields showing up rather well on the SLAR returns. However, these overflights soon came to an end after Francis Gary Powers' Lockheed U-2 was shot down on May Day 1960.

The SLAR was a highly valued asset to the US Army, which introduced the Grumman OV-1B Mohawk into service in 1961 with the SLAR-capable variant commencing monitoring of the Korean Demilitarised Zone in South Korea during 1963. The Mohawk's Motorola AN/APS-94 SLAR was fitted with a Motorola AN/APN-129 moving target indicator (MTI) to identify trucks and other vehicles. The SLAR's main role was surveillance and could monitor a swathe of land 62 miles (100km) of each side of the aircraft track. Resolution (ie, the distance between two objects before they can be shown as separate) varied with distance, with 260ft (80m) at 6 miles (10km) but deteriorating to 1,300ft (400m) at 31 miles (50km).

The Mohawk came into its own during the Vietnam War, allowing equipment concealed under foliage to be detected and targeted. The system was also used extensively in Europe and would have provided valuable information had the Cold War turned hot. On retiring the Mohawk, the capability was maintained by the Airborne Reconnaissance Low (ARL) platform that comprised fitting a SLAR and other sensors to a de Havilland Canada DASH-7 airliner to produce the EO-5C. This featured the latest development in radar sensors, the synthetic aperture radar (SAR). This is a technique that produces fine-resolution images, almost photographic quality, from a radar system of limited resolution. The radar should be moving, preferably in a straight line, and builds up its image from sequential scans, which are processed to produce the results. Some of the images are remarkable.

As they developed radars and signal processing systems, engineers discovered that objects smaller than geographical features, such as buildings and vehicles could be resolved on radar. Rather than being troubled by clutter and fast cars, the combination of SAR and MTI techniques formed the basis of an excellent surveillance and eventually target identification system. Thus Assault Breaker was created.

Assault Breaker was a US programme that evolved into the Precision Location and Strike System (PLSS) intended to counter any Soviet invasion of Western Europe. Assault Breaker used high-flying aircraft to view the battlefield with radar, allowing the locations of Warsaw Pact tanks and other vehicles

The Grumman OV-1B Mohawk was a STOL reconnaissance aircraft deployed by the US Army and Marine Corps. When fitted with the Motorola AN/APS-94 SLAR (in the large box under the starboard side of the forward fuselage) it could monitor large areas of the battlefield and, in Vietnam, detect vehicles under the forest canopy. It could also be armed, much to the chagrin of the USAF. (Blue Envoy Collection)

One project aimed at Assault Breaker was the Pave Mover, which comprised General Dynamics F-111E, 67-0115, with a ground-mapping radar in a ventral pod. The radar data was transmitted to a ground station for analysis as the F-111E lacked the capacity to handle processing. (Blue Envoy Collection)

Altitude = Range. By flying high, along, or just behind the forward line of own troops (FLOT), the SLAR could see deep into enemy territory. Helicopter or light aircraft-mounted radars had the benefit of working directly with the ground forces, reducing the sensor to shooter time. (Author)

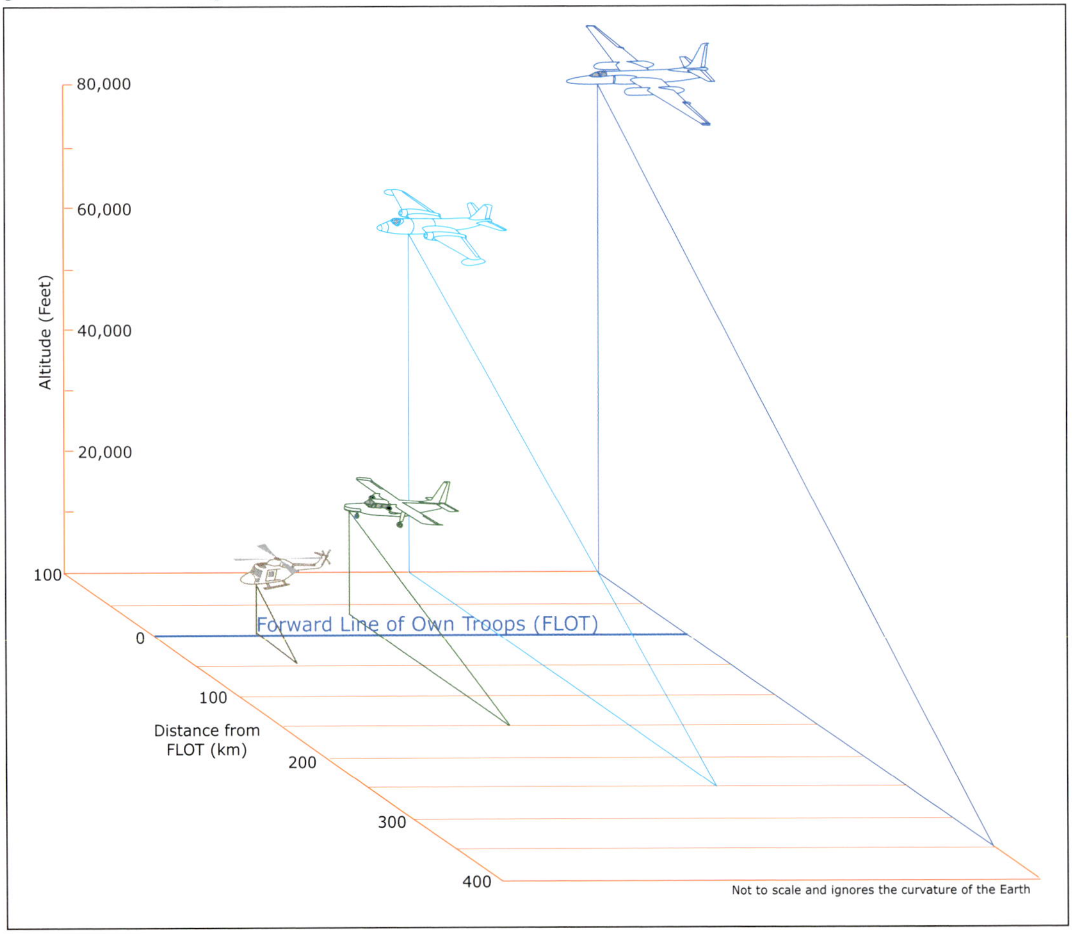

to be passed to ground stations thus allowing artillery, missiles and strike aircraft with smart munitions to 'attrit' them. The initial tests, conducted with a General Dynamics F-111 carrying the Pave Mover radar system that combined SAR and MTI, showed great promise. A higher-flying platform was preferred, however, and the USAF just happened to have one.

The plan for PLSS was to have a SAR-equipped Lockheed U-2R (called at the time 'TR-1' for Tactical Reconnaissance) orbiting west of the forward edge of the battlefield in West Germany and transferring the data to direct strikes against the advancing Soviet battlegroups. Then the Berlin Wall fell.

The TR-1s stayed in Europe, housed in the largest hardened aircraft shelters ever built (Swiss cavern hangars don't count), were renamed U-2Rs and conducted the usual U-2R activities until 1991. However, the effort was not wasted. The systems and technology developed for PLSS was transferred to a US Army/USAF programme that became known as Joint STARS (Surveillance Target Attack Radar System).

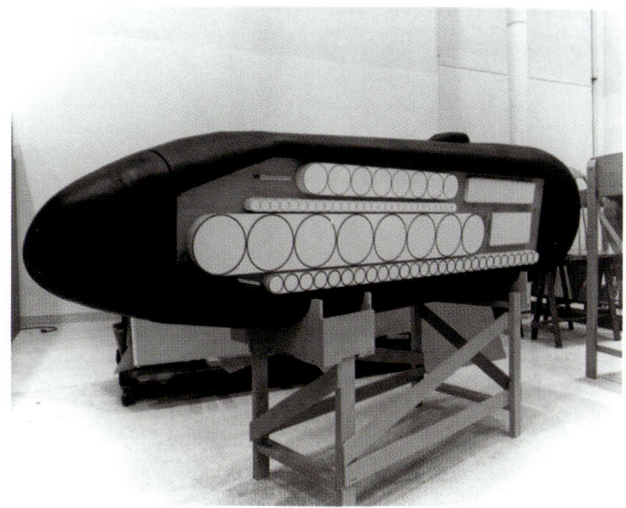

Right: This peculiar-looking item is a mock-up of the radar antenna from the nose of the Lockheed TR-1. Intended for the Precision Location and Strike System, the radar was the sensor portion of the USAF's Assault Breaker programme. (Blue Envoy Collection)

Below: Lockheed U-2S, 80-1083 landing at RAF Fairford. The extended nose houses the ASARS-2A (Advanced Synthetic Aperture Radar System 2A) while the large dorsal pod encloses the antenna for a Senior Span satellite datalink. Before upgrading to U-2S standard, the U-2R was known as TR-1 when assigned to stand-off reconnaissance in Europe in the early 1980s. (Chris Lofting)

Grumman Aerospace was, in 1985, awarded the contract to develop Joint STARS and was in the midst of its development when, in August 1990, Saddam Hussein invaded Kuwait. The two JSTARS development aircraft, designated E-8A, were undergoing trials when the balloon went up and would soon be pitched into operations.

The system comprised an AN/APY-7 SLAR installed in a 40ft (12.2m) long 'canoe' under the forward fuselage of a Boeing 707. The canoe houses a 24 ft (7.3 m) active electronically scanned array side-looking airborne radar antenna that allowed the JSTARS to monitor enemy manoeuvres from a distance. The radar operates in moving target indicator and SAR mode and can differentiate between tracked vehicles such as tanks and wheeled vehicles such as trucks and armoured cars. This capability allows the relevant ordnance to be selected and the target attrited in the most efficient manner. JSTARS is to the ground war what AEW is to the air war.

Britain's armed forces also saw the need for an airborne battlefield management system for use over West Germany and during 1978 a requirement, GSR 3956, was drawn up for a battlefield surveillance system. This would, via SAR and MTI technology, provide a radar picture of Warsaw Pact armoured formations up to 30 miles (48km) beyond the forward edge of the battlefield area (FEBA). This became known as the Corps Airborne STand-Off Radar (CASTOR) and the data gathered by the radar would be transmitted to a ground station for analysis and distribution. By 1983, a Thorn-EMI X-band sideways looking synthetic aperture radar (SAR) was installed in the bomb bay of Canberra WT327 for trials.

Taken into service during *Desert Shield* and subsequent operations to liberate Kuwait, the Boeing E-8A JSTARS was a force multiplier that pretty much did for the ground war what AWACS had done for the air war. The key to JSTARS is the 24ft (7.3m) long antenna for the AN/APY-7 radar under the forward fuselage. Based on its performance in Kuwait, the US Department of Defense ordered the E-8C production model. (Blue Envoy Collection)

During the CASTOR programme, a test radar was installed in the bomb bay of English Electric Canberra B(I)8 WT327. The Radar Research Establishment had used WT327 for various trials but to test the high-altitude aspects of the SLAR for CASTOR, the Canberra was invaluable. (Blue Envoy Collection)

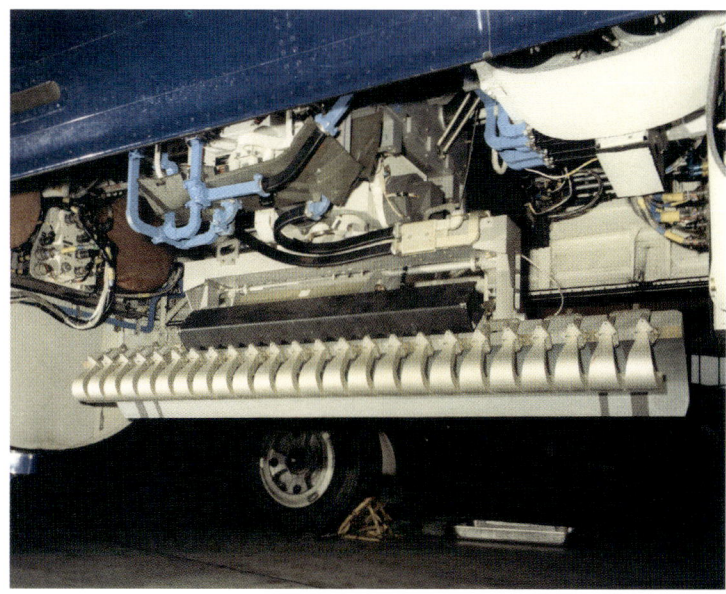

With the dielectric panels removed for maintenance, the 24 'horns' of the SLAR's antenna is exposed. This radar was flown in Canberra WT327 for trials under the CASTOR programme. (Blue Envoy Collection)

Not an AEW Defender but ZG989, the Britten-Norman Islander-ASTOR was used for trials of the Thorn-EMI ground surveillance with the British Army. In addition to the enlarged radome, ZG989 was fitted with a heat exchanger on the starboard side of the rear fuselage. (Blue Envoy Collection)

During 1982, a second CASTOR system was undergoing flight trials in the nose of a Britten-Norman Turbine Islander G-DLRA/ZG989. This version was aimed at the Army, which already operated the Turbine Islander as the Defender and would operate at lower altitude than the Thorn-EMI system in the Canberra. The system installed in the Islander comprised an I-band 360° scanning system from Ferranti for comparative trials against the Thorn-EMI systems. Realistically, the Army only needed to 'see' as far into enemy territory as its artillery systems could reach whereas the RAF needed deeper observation to identify targets for its strike aircraft. Having proved that the principle was feasible, both projects were subsequently cancelled.

In 1987, the Army's CASTOR requirement for a battlefield surveillance radar was merged with an RAF requirement for a new ground-mapping SAR. A requirement for an Airborne Stand-Off Radar (ASTOR) was issued as Staff Requirement (Land/Air) 925 covering a battlefield surveillance system with invitations to tender issued in 1994. Raytheon's bid was selected in 1999, based around a modified ASARS-2 radar that would prove to have higher resolution than the ASARS-2 fitted to the Lockheed

The Ferranti CASTOR radar was tested during 1984 on another Islander, G-DLRA. The verdict was that a higher-flying, deeper-looking system was required, leading to the Raytheon Sentinel R1. (Terry Panopalis Collection)

U-2S reconnaissance aircraft. The radar and systems were to be carried aloft by a Bombardier Global Express bizjet with five airframes ordered, plus the associated ground stations, to enter service in 2005. The radar was a dual-mode SAR/MTI with swathe and spot modes plus the capability to combine SAR and MTI to provide tracking of moving targets. It effectively gave the RAF the same capability as the USAF's E-8A in a much smaller aircraft.

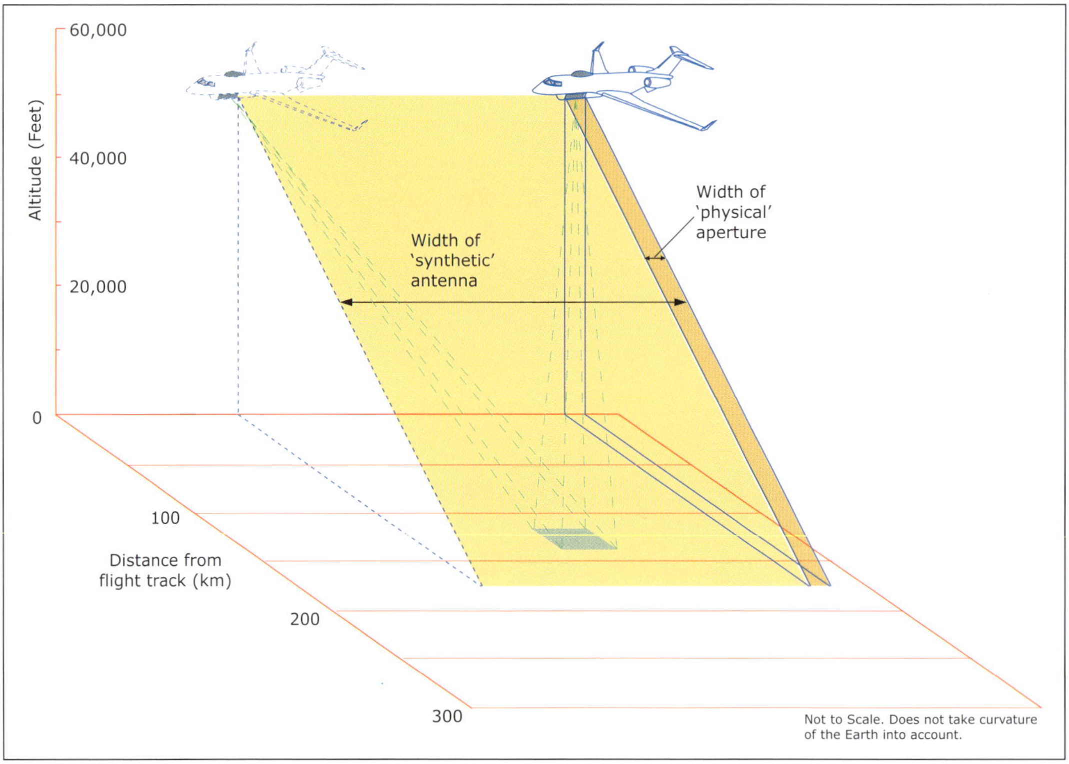

A synthetic aperture radar (SAR) works by building a 'picture' from a series of radar returns collected normal to the flightline to provide a highly detailed image of the ground below. The ASARS radar on Sentinel R1 could work in wide area or spot scan. (Author)

ASTOR entered service as the Sentinel R1 in 2008 with V (Army Co-operation) Sqn at RAF Waddington, the main base for the RAF's intelligence, surveillance, target acquisition, and reconnaissance (ISTAR) assets. The fifth aircraft, ZJ693, was placed in storage in May 2017 leaving four Sentinels to soldier on. The Sentinel fleet operated in Afghanistan from 2008 until 2018, Libya in 2011 and from 2015 deployed in support of coalition forces fighting against Daesh in Iraq and Syria. Then in one of many controversial penny-pinching acts inflicted on the armed services since 2010, the British government announced its intention to withdraw and sell the Sentinels.

The Sentinel fleet had not received the regular upgrades and modifications to keep the Sentinels at the cutting edge of ground surveillance. By late 2020, the cost of making these upgrades across the fleet was deemed prohibitive and the Sentinels were withdrawn from service in March 2021. When Russia invaded Ukraine in February 2022, alongside the many AEW aircraft operating along the western borders of Ukraine and Belarus was the Boeing E-8A JSTARS. The United Kingdom has, like all NATO countries, provided much support to Ukraine but how much more effective could that support have been if a pair of Sentinels were 'on the job'?

As noted in Chapter 9, Soviet Frontovaya Aviatsiya (Frontal Aviation) chose to develop a tactical AEW platform based on the Antonov An-72 *Coaler*. Similarly, when a ground surveillance platform along the lines of JSTARS or ASTOR was required, Frontal Aviation also opted for a *Coaler*-based machine. Developed under the codename *Tsirkon* (Zircon), the An-72R (Razvedchik) featured an extended fin fillet, but the main modification was a pair of long fairings extending along the length of the fuselage sides from the wing root leading edge to just short of the tail cone. These fairings housed dielectric panels for antennae and systems that allowed the An-72R to detect and classify ground targets, whose locations were then passed on to tactical strike aircraft.

The An-72R, like the An-71 in the AEW role, showed the difference between the Soviet/Russian and US/NATO approach to surveillance and target identification, with the Soviet/Russian systems being

The RAF's decades of involvement in ground mapping/radar reconnaissance development culminated in the Raytheon Sentinel R1. The long ventral canoe houses the antenna for the ASARS radar while the dorsal 'hump' covers the satellite communications antenna. (MOD/Open Government Licence)

tactically oriented. Development of the An-72R, like most advanced projects in the Russian Federation, came to an abrupt halt as the structures of the former Soviet Union collapsed.

In the ashes of the Soviet Union, military aviation development continued, albeit at a reduced rate especially once the new millennium began. The Beriev A-50 *Mainstay* is described in Chapter 9 and while it possessed a maritime surveillance capability, its use in the battlefield surveillance role against ground targets was poor. The A-50's successor, the A-100, is thought to include an improved battlefield surveillance capability in its Premier radar, with the ability to track surface as well as airborne targets.

While there appears to be no dedicated fixed wing battlefield surveillance aircraft, the Russian Army has been testing a helicopter in the role. The Kamov Ka-35 *Helix* is a land-based version of the Ka-31R maritime AEW platform. The E-801 *Oko* (Eye) radar on the AEW machine has been replaced with the 15S100.10, optimised for detection and tracking of ground targets.

L'Orchidée

France's army wanted its ground-surveillance systems nearby and opted for a helicopter-borne radar system called Orchidée. The US and UK had dabbled with radars on helicopters with the Sikorsky YEH-60B Blackhawk, configured to carry the US Army's Stand Off Target Acquisition System (SOTAS) and a proposal for a battlefield radar on a British Army Air Corps Westland Lynx. Both services deemed the helicopter too expensive to operate compared with a fixed wing aircraft such as the Islander proposed for CASTOR.

France's Aviation Légère de l'Armée de Terre Land Army Light Aviation (ALAT) on the other hand were the French Army's air arm and happy to use a helicopter. The prototype involved fitting the radar in an Aerospatiale AS330 Puma but since the Aerospatiale AS332 Super Puma Mk II was entering ALAT service in the late 1980s, this was the type selected to carry a pulse Doppler radar to detect and track vehicles and helicopters up to a range of 93 miles (150km). The system became known as Orchidée, an acronym for Observatoire Radar Cohérent Héliporté d'Investigation (Heliborne Coherent Radar Observatory for Investigation).

Despite being cancelled in 1990, the Orchidée system was dug out to serve with French forces during the liberation of Kuwait. The Orchidée, mounted on an SA330 Puma, was subsequently replaced by HORIZON. (Blue Envoy Collection)

The large rectangular antenna was mounted where the helicopter's tail boom met the cabin and rotated clear of the helicopter's underside but folded aft and up through 90° to lift the antenna clear of the ground. By the time the prototype Orchidée flew in 1988, a SAR developed by SEB SA was installed in the Super Puma to improve the system's target identification capability.

Like the USAF's E-8A, Orchidée went to war while still in development serving in Operation *Daguet*, the liberation of Kuwait in February 1991, finding a niche as part of a hunter/killer team seeking out Iraqi armoured formations that would be attacked by ALAT Gazelle or US Army Apache anti-armour helicopters.

After the Gulf War, the Orchidée received a new Thompson CSF radar, which replaced the SEB unit. This led to the whole system being renamed HORIZON, another acronym for Hélicoptère d'Observation Radar et d'Investigation sur ZONe (Radar Observation and Investigation Helicopter on ZONe). In its latest guise, the Horizon system is modular and can be installed in the ALAT's Eurocopter AS532UL Cougar.

Radar reconnaissance and battlefield surveillance systems have come a long way since the initial H2S sets were carried over Germany in the first months of 1943. In the decades since, what used to be called clutter has become valuable intelligence, especially once synthetic aperture radars were developed, which allow almost photographic quality images to be acquired at long range, even from space. Coupled with moving target indicators and especially computer processing, radar reconnaissance systems such as the E-8 and Sentinel could detect and track vehicles but also identify the class of vehicle, possibly even down to the type of tank. Impressive systems indeed, and for any armed forces that describe themselves as first rate, an essential weapon on their armoury.

The second generation of battlefield surveillance for the Aviation Légère de l'Armée de Terre (ALAT) was HORIZON. Seen here carried by a Eurocopter AS532UL Cougar, the system is modular and can be fitted to most of the AS532UL utility variants of the ALAT's Cougars. (Blue Envoy Collection)

Conclusion

The 1st Duke of Wellington famously said: 'All the business of war, indeed all the business of life, is to endeavour to find out what you don't know from what you do: that is what is called "guessing what's on the other side of the hill"'.

Airborne early warning aircraft allow commanders to see what is on the other side of the hill, and what's over the horizon. The technical problems associated with AEW were finally overcome in the 1980s and the AEW platforms of today are a fraction of the size of their predecessors. They also possess capabilities beyond the wildest dreams of a fighter controller directing Mosquitos in a cold and draughty Wellington. We have come a long way from the Wellington to the Wedgetail.

Similarly, the less well-known battlefield surveillance role provides the commanders of ground forces a 'God's eye' view of the battle and allows timely and effective deployments of troops and equipment, not to mention much improved targeting.

As a force multiplier, the presence of AEW has had a positive impact on air battles since the early 1960s, be it the Warning Stars over Vietnam and their contribution to MiG shootdowns or the Israeli Hawkeyes over the Bekaa Valley in 1982. Lack of AEW on the other hand, probably contributed to the loss of HMS *Sheffield* and the SS *Atlantic Conveyor* in the Falklands War. In the land war, the contribution made by the E-8s during Russia's war on Ukraine is by necessity confidential but their use in the Middle East, particularly in the liberation of Kuwait resulted in a quick defeat for Iraqi land forces.

These systems – war-winning systems – have been viewed as less important in the order of battle, especially by recent British governments. The country that first developed and fielded an AEW platform gave away (literally) both capabilities, but the pigeons came home to roost in February 2022. There may still be time to address these short-sighted decisions. There was a widely held view amongst British Army officers during the Cold War: 'Fight to the Rhine, then call Downing Street'. In other words, ask permission to release nuclear weapons. The AEW and battlefield surveillance types described herein would have delayed, if not prevented, that phone call. Hopefully that call will never be made.

Appendix 1

Radar Basics

Radar (RAdio Detection And Ranging) uses a radio frequency (RF) signal emitted by a transmitter via an antenna and is reflected back from an object (the return) to a receiver via an antenna. By measuring the time taken for this round trip, the distance (range) to an object can be determined.

Pulsed radars emit a series of RF signals with a period of silence between. This period of silence is used to detect return signals and measures range but not speed.

A pulse-Doppler radar uses the Doppler effect to determine target range and velocity. Pulse-Doppler radars require a coherent signal and use elaborate processing to produce that signal's output. Pulse-Compression radars utilise signal processing to improve range resolution by modulating the transmitted pulse and correlating this with the received pulse.

Continuous Wave (CW) radars transmit a constant signal at a known frequency and the return is analysed for frequency changes. These changes are caused by the movement of the target and the Doppler

Comet IV testbed, XW626, with the radome removed to expose the 8 x 6ft (2.44 x 1.82m) folded-focus Cassegrain antenna of the Marconi-Elliott radar. This antenna would be replaced by an offset parabolic type on the definitive Nimrod AEW3. It was one of many changes that greatly improved the radar's performance. (Via Terry Panopalis)

effect. CW radars are mainly used in the detection and tracking of moving objects and can give precise measurement of an object's speed, however they cannot measure range.

Frequency Modulated Continuous Wave radar (FMCW) uses a frequency that varies over time and compares the transmitted frequency with the received and therefore can be used to determine range and speed. FMCW normally required separate transmit and receive antennas, but Frequency Modulated Interrupted Continuous Wave radar (FMICW) allows a single antenna to be used by interrupting the signal. One major benefit of FMICW radar is that signal processing is easier than with a pulse-Doppler radar, reducing the computer power required compared with pulse-Doppler systems.

To operate in an early warning role, an aircraft using a pulse radar may have an airborne moving target indicator (AMTI), which is used to identify a return against the clutter of the ground return. On static ground-based radars with moving target indicators (MTI) this can be done with Doppler analysis, but if the transmitter and receiver are moving then a Doppler shifted return will be received from the ground due to relative movement. The benefit of Pulse-Doppler and FMICW radars is that they do not require AMTI.

Since the 1990s a new type of radar system has appeared, the active electronically scanned array (AESA) radar. This is a variant of the phased array radar that steers the radar emissions electronically allowing the antenna to be fixed. This works by using an array of transmit/receive modules on the face of the antenna, with each module directed to transmit (and receive) the radar signal. This allows a flat plate antenna to cover a sector of up to 120° of arc. Interestingly the Beriev *Mainstay* has used not only mechanically scanned (A-50M) and electronically scanned (A-50EI) antennas, but a combination of both in the A-100, which scans mechanically in azimuth but electronically in elevation.

It appears that despite the AESA becoming the antenna of choice, how the antennae are fitted to the aircraft are many and varied.

Appendix 2

FASS and FMICW – Britain's Preference

The Fore and Aft Scanner System (FASS) was the configuration of choice for British AEW designers from 1945 until the end of the road in 1987. ASR writers and AEW system developers believed that putting the radar antennas in the nose and tail of the aircraft allowed the radar to view the world unrestricted by airframe blanking. Unlike the rotodome of the E-2 Hawkeye, the smaller scanners, sweeping through 184° arcs, could also be stabilised in pitch and roll. With its rotodome, the Hawkeye was restricted to flat turns while stabilised scanners allowed a more comfortable environment for the operators and simplified the pilot's task as the aircraft orbited on patrol as the aircraft banked in its turns.

FASS worked by having each of the scanners covering an arc of 184° in turn. The forward scanner swept from port to starboard transmitting and receiving as it did so. When the antenna reached its limit of travel, using the last 2° of each traverse to decelerate, the radar system 'changed ends' to the aft scanner that began its sweep from starboard to port and at the end of each sweep the antenna rapidly returned to its start position to begin its next sweep, thus providing a 360° uninterrupted radar picture. One benefit of the FASS configuration was that the antennae could be stabilised allowing the aircraft to perform banked turns, unlike the Hawkeye with its rotodome. Ultimately the electronically scanned phased-array antenna reduced the need for mechanical scanning and stabilisation on AEW radars.

However, FASS might just have the last laugh as types such as the Gulfstream G550CAEW are fitted with a FASS, coupled with conformal arrays on the sides of the fuselage. Nimrod AEW3 was just another example of the perils of being an early adopter.

To test the Marconi radar, Hawker Siddeley at Woodford in 1977, converted former BOAC de Havilland Comet 4 G-APDS into radar testbed XW626. Only one scanner was installed, in the nose, with the other external changes being the intakes for heat exchangers on the rear fuselage and a Nimrod-style fin fillet. (Blue Envoy Collection)

Glossary

ACI	Airborne Control and Interception
AEW	Airborne Early Warning
AI	Air Interception
AMTI	Airborne Moving Target Indicator
ASCC	Air Standards Coordination Committee
ASR	Air Staff Requirement
AST	Air Staff Target
ASV	Air-to-Surface Vessel
ASW	Anti-Submarine Warfare
AUW	All-Up-Weight
AWACS	Airborne Warning And Control System
BAE Systems	Formed in 1999 from former BAe (British Aerospace) and Marconi and General Electric Company
BAC	British Aircraft Corporation
DRDO	Defence Research and Development Organisation
FAA	Fleet Air Arm
FASS	Fore and Aft Scanner System
FMICW	Frequency Modulated Interrupted Continuous Wave
GSR	General Staff Requirement
GST	General Staff Target
HSA	Hawker Siddeley Aviation
JSTARS	Joint Surveillance Target Attack Radar System
MEASL	Marconi Elliott Avionics Systems Limited
MOD	Ministry of Defence (UK)
MSA	Mission Systems Avionics
OR	Operational Requirement
PLSS	Precision Location and Strike System
RAF	Royal Air Force
RN	Royal Navy
RRE	Radar Research Establishment
TRE	Telecommunications Research Establishment
USAF	United States Air Force
USN	United States Navy

Bibliography

Gibson, C. *The Air Staff and AEW*, Blue Envoy Press (2012)
Gibson, C, *The Admiralty and AEW*, Blue Envoy Press (2011)
Gibson, C. *Vickers VC10, AEW, Pofflers and Other Unbuilt Variants*, Blue Envoy Press (2009)
Gibson, C. *Battle Flight*, Crecy Publishing (2018)
Gibson, C. *Typhoon to Typhoon*, Crecy publishing (2018)
Gordon, Y. and Komissarov, D. *Russian and Soviet Special Mission Aircraft*, Crecy Publishing (2022)
Shaw, I. and Santana, S. *Beyond the Horizon: The History of AEW&C Aircraft*, Harpia Publishing (2014)
Hirst, M. *Airborne Early Warning: Design, Development and Operations*, Bloomsbury Publishing (1983)

Journals
Flight International, Flight Global/DVV Media, various issues
International Air Power Review, Aerospace Publishing, various issues
World Air Power Journal, Aerospace Publishing, various issues

Other books you might like:

Modern Military Aircraft Series, Vol. 3

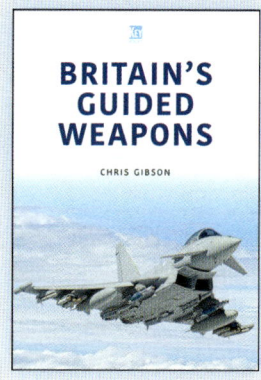

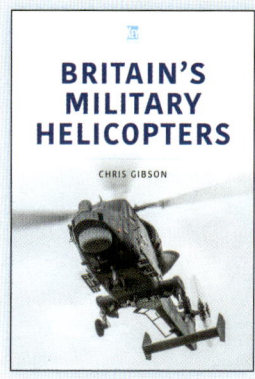

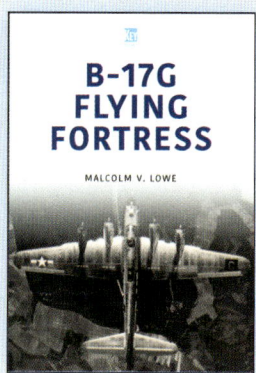

Modern Military Aircraft Series, Vol. 6

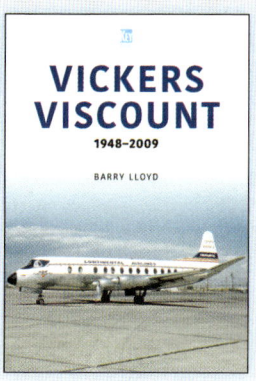

Modern Military Aircraft Series, Vol. 4

Historic Military Aircraft Series, Vol. 11

Historical Commercial Aircraft Series, Vol. 16

For our full range of titles please visit:
shop.keypublishing.com/books

VIP Book Club

Sign up today and receive
TWO FREE E-BOOKS

Be the first to find out about our forthcoming book releases and receive exclusive offers.

Register now at **keypublishing.com/vip-book-club**

Our VIP Book Club is a 100% spam-free zone, and we will never share your email with anyone else. You can read our full privacy policy at: privacy.keypublishing.com